YPS

YESHIVA PIRCHEI SHOSHANIM
ישיבה פרחי שושנים

Pirchei Publishing
164 Village Path / P.O. Box 708
Lakewood, New Jersey 08701
(732) 370-3344
www.shulchanaruch.com

Product Produced & Compiled by YPS:
Rabbi Shaul Danyiel & Rabbi Ari Montanari
www.lionsden.info/YPS

Table of Contents

An Overview

Rehov Beit Vegan 99, Yerushalayim 02.644.6376

164 Village Path, Lakewood NJ 08701 732.370.3344 fax 1.877.Pirchei (732.367.8168)

A Short Overview of the Construction of the Hebrew Language

(In 100 words or less)

The Hebrew Language is built around three-letter root words, each of which forms the core of the nouns, verbs, and other parts of speech relating to the root. The nuances of eating, feeding, being fed, digesting, being eaten, gluttony, slaughtering knife, devouring, eatable and indeed the word "food" itself, are all created by the addition of predictable and consistent prefixes, suffixes, infixes (inserted letters), and vowels which attach to a single, unique, three-letter root (*shoresh*). **The keys to understanding are: identifying the root and identifying the function of the letters and vowels attaching to the root.**

This book can teach you to do that, in just a few hours.

Abbreviations

The following abbreviations are used throughout this book:

G	=	Gender (masculine or feminine)	M	=	Male	F =	Female
N	=	Number (singular or plural)	S	=	Singular	Pl =	Plural
D	=	Definitiveness ("the")					
T	=	Tense (past, present, future)					
P	=	Person: (1st = I, we; 2nd = you [S], you [Pl]; 3rd = he, she [S], they, them [Pl]					
C	=	Common for both M and F					

Parts of Speech

I Noun

- A noun is a person, place, thing, or concept. In Hebrew, It **always** has gender and number.

II Pronoun

- A non-definitive word that substitutes for a noun (i.e. "it"), "It" must agree in person, gender, and number with the noun it replaces.

A. Possessive Pronoun

- A possessive pronoun shows ownership. It either takes the place of a noun or is attached to a noun.

B. Demonstrative Pronoun

- A word that identifies a specific object, i.e., "this" book.

III Adjective

- An adjective describes *how* or *what* is the noun. In Hebrew, it must agree with the noun in gender, number and definitiveness. A noun's adjective follows the noun and has the same gender as the *true* gender of the noun.

A. Definite Article

- A definitive article limits or specifies. In English the word "the" is the definitive article. In Hebrew the prefix "ה" is the sign of the definitive article.

B. Indefinite Article

- In Hebrew, there is no sign for the indefinite article. All nouns are assumed to be indefinite unless they are made definite.

IV Verb

- A Verb expresses an action, a state of being, or a condition. The verb indicates the time reference of the sentence - (past, present, or future). The verb must agree with the subject noun in gender, number, and person.

Infinitive

- In English the infinitive is the "to" form of the verb (i.e. *to learn, to daven*). In Hebrew, it is characterized by a "ל" prefix preceding the verb root as a relative makor vowel pattern.

V Adverb

- An adverb describes, qualifies or limits a verb, adjective or another adverb. In Hebrew, it does not have to agree with the verb in gender, number, person, or definitiveness. *He learns quickly.* *"Quickly"* is the adverb.

VI Preposition

- A connective word that joins nouns or pronouns to the verb. A preposition shows relationship (i.e. *with, at from, of, by*).

VII Conjunction

- A conjunction connects words, phrases and clauses (i.e. *and, or, but*).

Parts of the Sentence

I Subject

- The subject of a sentence is a noun or pronoun that does, causes, or receives the action of the verb. It has gender, number, and person.

II Object

- The direct object of a sentence receives the action of the verb.

A. Direct Object

- The direct object answers the question "who" or "what" of the verb. It must come directly after the verb (ex. *I guarded a Sefer Torah.* *"Sefer Torah"* is the direct object.)

B. Indirect Object

- An indirect object receives the action of the verb indirectly (ex. *Shimon gave the book to me.* *"To me"* is the indirect object.)

C. Object of the Preposition

- A prepositional phrase consists of a preposition and a noun or pronoun, with or without adjectives. The noun or pronoun is the object of the preposition (ex. *Moshe placed the book on the table. Shimon learned in Yeshiva. "Table"* and *"Yeshiva"* are objects of the preposition.)

III Predicate

- The predicate is the portion of the sentence containing the verb. A predicate says something about the subject of the sentence.

Lesson 1

Rehov Beit Vegan 99, Yerushalayim 02.644.6376

1091 River Ave., Lakewood NJ 08701 732.370.3344 fax 1.877.Pirchei (732.367.8168)

Chapter One
The Hebrew Alphabet

Getting to know the Hebrew Letters

Before we start, familiarize yourself with the letters. These are the four basic styles that you will find. This course focuses on advancing one's reading comprehension. It is expected that you already know the basic pronunciation of the letters. Take your time.

Regular	Block Print	Script	Rashi Script
א	א	וc	ऻ
ב	ב	ə	३
ג	ג	ċ	૮
ד	ד	ʒ	૧
ה	ה	ற	౧
ו	ו	ı	า
ז	ז	ੇ	ſ
ח	ח	ŋ	೧
ט	ט	૮	౮
י	י	᾽	᾽
כ	כ	ɔ	೨
ך	ך	₽	٦
ל	ל	ſ	১
מ	מ	א	೧
ם	ם	ρ	೦
נ	נ	J	১
ן	ן			١
ס	ס	₀	೦
ע	ע	૪	౮
פ	פ	౧	೨
ף	ף	ſ	٩
צ	צ	₃	১
ץ	ץ	૪	౮
ק	ק	ρ	೨
ר	ר	১	১
ש	ש	ℓ	೮
ת	ת	೨	೧

Chapter Two

Section One

Let's Begin

The Hebrew Alphabet has 23[1] consonants. Five of the consonants also have a final form, when they appear as a last letter of a word, for a total of 28 letters **any** of the 28 letters **can** function as a *Root*[2] letter of a word. The 28 letters can be subdivided into four categories according to their potential function(s).

Category 1—Root letters only

Category 2—Root letters or Prefixes

Category 3—Root letters, or Prefixes or Suffixes

Category 4—Root letters, or Prefixes, or Suffixes or Infixes

Section Two

All 28 Letters can function as root letters.

1. **Root letters only**

   This category consists of 12 letters, which can **only** function as root letters in a word.

THESE LETTERS ARE:

(שׁ, ר, ק, צ, פ, ע, ס) (ט, ח, ז) (ד, ג)

---

1 שׁ and שׂ are being counted as different consonants

2 **Root:** שרשׁ (*shoresh*): The three primary letter structure of a word (usually a verb) with no vowels conveying a primal meaning.

Examples

   a.   לְפַשֵׁט   The root letters must be פשט

   b.   וַיִּשְׂרְפוּ   The root letters must be שרפ

   c.   וְרָחַל   The root letters must be רחל

2.   **Root letters or Prefixes**

This category consists of four letters, which can serve two functions. They may be root letters or they may function as a prefix (before the first root letter). If one of these four letters follows any letter in category 1, or category 3, or any other letter in category 2, then, it may no longer be a prefix letter and must be a root letter. [**Note**: A word may have more than one prefix].

THESE LETTERS ARE:

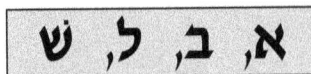

א, ב, ל, שׁ

A) א as a prefix is a sign of the first person future tense masculine and feminine singular, translating to *I will*.

Examples

a.   אֶהְיֶה   The א prefix added to the root היה (*be*) = *I will be*.

b.   וַיֵּצֵא   Here the א must be a root letter.

c.   וְאֶרְאֶה   Here the ו is a prefix and also the first א is *I will*, while the א after ר must be a root letter. ראה (*look*)

d.   אֶרֶץ   א is the first root letter. ארץ (*land* or *earth*)

e.   אָרוּץ   The א prefix added to the root רוצ (*run*) = *I will run*.

f.   וַיֹּאחֲזוּ   Here the prefix pre-empts the א ability to be a future tense prefix making the root אחז (*acquire* or *hold* or *grab*)

[We must remember the letters relative position is only one factor to be considered when deciding the function of a particular letter. Other letters in close proximity and vowelling patterns, also, play a major role in determining a letters function.]

B) בּ as a prefix is a preposition translating to *in* or *with* and having five or six secondary possible translations.

Examples

a.   בַּלֶּחֶם   בּ as prefix translates to *with the bread.* לחם (*bread*)

b.   בְּבָתֵּיכֶם   The double בּ tells us to use the first בּ as a prefix and the second בּ as the first root letter of בתי (*house*) and כֶם the possessive pronoun suffix (*your*). Translation *In your houses.*

c   שֹׂבֵעַ   In this word the בּ must be a root letter as it follows another letter in category 1. שבע (*satiated*)

C) ל as a prefix serves two functions:

- *Sign of infinitive*: When the ל is a prefix before the verb root in the form of the relative *makor*, the ל functions as the infinitive of the verb root and its *binian* root will be determined by vowelling (extra letter) patterns.

- *Prepositional prefix*: When the ל is a prefix before a noun or object preposition, the ל functions as a preposition, meaning *to* or *for*.

Examples

a.   לְמִצְרָיִם   Means to Egypt. With the ל as a prepositional prefix.

b.   לְיַעֲקֹב   Means to or for Jacob. With the ל as a prepositional prefix.

c.   לָהֶם   Means to them or for them. With the ל as a prepositional prefix to an object pronoun.

d.   לְךָ   Means to you or for you, masculine singular second person as a prepositional prefix.

e.   לִרְאוֹת   The ל is a sign of the infinitive meaning to see. For the root ראה.

f.   לֵאמוֹר   The ל is a sign of the verb infinitive meaning to say. For the root אמר.

g.   לִסְבֹּל   The ל prefix is the infinitive ל while the second ל must be root letter.

h.   וַיֵּלְכוּ   The ל must be a root letter with the י as a prefix the ל can no longer be a prefix letter.

D) שֶׁ as a prefix translates to *that, which* or *since*. It is a short form of the word אֲשֶׁר:

Examples

a. שֶׁיֹּאכַל   That which he will eat.

b. שֶׁאֵין   Since there is not

c. כָּשֵׁר   In this word the שׁ must be a root letter.

3.   **Root letters, or Prefixes, or Suffixes**

This category consists of five letters, which can serve three functions. They may be root letters; or they may function as a prefix (before the first root letter); or they may function as a suffix (after the last root letter). A good general rule to follow is: When one of these five letters appears before or after a definite root letter, it is probably serving its prefix or suffix function, and not as a root letter. When one of these five letters appears between any other of the letters, it will be a root letter. Also included in this category, as suffixes or root letters, are the final three letters ך, ם, ן. See prefix, suffix, and infix chart in lesson 15 to see how these five letters can function, as each serves multiple functions.

THESE LETTERS ARE:

ה, כ, מ, נ, ת

Examples

a. וַיֹּאמֶר   The מ must be a root letter with the א and ר.

b. כָּחֲשׁוּ   The כ can either be a prefix letter or root letter, in this case it's a root letter in the word כחש

c. וְזָנַבְתֶּם   The נ must be a root letter sandwiched between ז and ב, which must be root letters.

d. מֵעֲבָדֶיךָ   The מ is most likely a prefix letter since it precedes three root letters and the ך at the end is most assuredly a letter suffix and not part of the root.

If ה, כ, מ, נ, ת are not locked into a position of having to be a root letter, than, the overwhelming majority of the time, they function as prefix or suffix letters.

4.   **Root letters, or Prefixes, or Suffixes, or Infixes**

This category consists of two letters (י and ו), which can serve four functions. They may be root letters; or they may function as a prefix (before the first root letter); or they may function as a suffix (after the last root letter); or they may function as an infix (a letter between two root letters that is not functioning as a root letter).

THESE LETTERS ARE:

ו , י

The ו (*holom*) can be written full as in בוא or without the actual ו, with the dot above the letter preceding the ו as in בֹא. The ו (*shurak*) can also be written full as in יוּתַן or without the actual ו and the *kubutz* below the letter preceding as in יֻתַן.

Examples

a.   וַיָמֻתוּ   The ו is a prefix as is יְ and the וּ is a suffix. The מֻ (the *mem*) with the *kubutz* represents the ו as a root letter, that has not been dropped from the root מות.

b.   וַיֹּאמֶר   The ו is a reversing prefix. *Vav.* And the י is a future tense prefix.

c.   גְדֹלוֹת   The ד with the *holom* is as if the word was written as גְדוֹל. The second *holom* ו is part of the feminine plural ending.

d.   יָקוּם   The יְ is a future prefix, and the וּ is a root letter.

Chapter Three

Vowels

As we saw above, the 23 letters in the Hebrew alphabet are all consonants. The symbols under the letter, and the characters וֹ and וּ following the letters, are called vowels. A consonant with its vowel, and often the consonant-vowel pair in combination with another consonant, form a syllable. Syllables follow rules, **not** sounds. A **syllable** is a letter or a group of letters that contain one long or short vowel **only**. Multiple sounds can combine to form single syllables. There are two types of vowels: short and long.

It is **imperative** to know the five long and short vowels instinctively, to be able to read, syllabalize, and pronounce words properly. The *sheva* (**׃**) in combination with a vowel,

for example ׃ ‎ ־ְ / ֱ: / ־ֲ is not considered a short or long vowel.

Long Vowels			Short Vowels	
קָמַץ	אָ		אַ	פַּתָּח
שׁוּרֻק	אוּ		אֻ	קֻבּוּץ
חִירִיק מָלֵא	אִי	The name of the vowel, if pronounced properly, contains the proper pronunciation of that vowel	אִ	חִירִיק חָסֵר
חוֹלָם	אֹ, אוֹ		אָ	קָמַץ קָטָן
צֵירֶה	אֵ		אֶ	סֶגוֹל

Rule 1: Long vowels always end a syllable. The letter with its vowel or *sheva* that follows a long vowel always begins a new syllable.

Rule 2: Short vowels with a letter always demand that the letter and vowel or *sheva* that follow the letter with the short vowel close the syllable.

A short quiz will follow the lesson on the *sheva*, incorporating the two sections into the check yourself quiz. Since the *sheva* is so intimately connected with the long and short vowels, examples will also be found at the end of the sections on *sheva*.

The Rules for analyzing words and breaking them down must be developed with time and practice, combining many factors in letter combinations, vowelling, and set patterns, that will be developed as we learn more of the text. This will enable you to sharpen your intuitive/knowledgeable analysis of words.

Most sections will end with a Self-Checking Quiz, but due to the many variables involved with word identification, this section has no Self-Checking Quiz.

Lesson 2

Rehov Beit Vegan 99, Yerushalayim 02.9920755
1091 River Ave. Village Path, Lakewood NJ 08701 732.370.3344 fax 1.877.Pirchei (732.367.8168)

Chapter One

Sheva Nach (נח) & Sheva Na (נע)

The Vertical Dots

The *sheva* (:) is half a vowel written as two vertical dots under the consonant. The rules for *sheva* are as follows:

Section One

1. **Sheva Nach (נח)**

    A. The *sheva nach* is silent (adds no sound to the letter it is under).

    B. A *sheva* under a consonant, following a consonant with a short vowel is a *sheva nach*.

        a. וַיִּקְרָא

        b. וַיַּבְדֵל

        c. יַבְדִּיל

    C. When two *shevas* follow each other in one word, the first *sheva* is always a *sheva nach*, and is following a short vowel.

        a. יִשְׁרְצוּ

        b. וְנִפְקְחוּ

        c. וְיִתְפְּרוּ

    D. A *sheva* at the end of a word is always a *sheva nach*.

        a. בְּתוֹךְ

        b. וְלַחֹשֶׁךְ

Section Two

1. **Sheva Na** (נע)

A. The *sheva na* is pronounced like a short *segol* (i.e. like the i in little).

B. The *sheva na* is not really a vowel, it is a half vowel, and does not need to be closed, and it is an inseparable part of the consonant and vowel that follow it. It must not be read as a separate syllable.

C. The *sheva* that appears under the first letter of a word is always a *sheva na*.
   a. בְּרֵאשִׁית
   b. פְּנֵי
   c. מְרַחֶפֶת

D. A consonant that follows another consonant with a long vowel always takes a *sheva na* and begins a syllable.
   a. וְתִירָשְׁךָ
   b. אוֹמְרִים
   c. יְמִינְךָ

E. When two *shevas* follow each other, the second is always a *sheva na*.
   a. יִשְׁרְצוּ
   b. וְנִפְקְחוּ
   c. וַיִּתְפְּרוּ

F. The *sheva na* appears under a letter with a *dagesh chazak*.
   a. הַמְּאֹרֹת
   b. הַגְּדֹלִים
   c. הַבְּהֵמָה

G. Where two identical letters follow each other in one word, the *sheva* under the first of the doubled letters is always a *sheva na* and pronounced as if the letter has a *dagesh*.
   a. הַלְלוּסָה
   b. יְבָרֶכְךָ
   c. הִנְנִי

Section Three

1.   Chataf Sheva

A *sheva* in combination with a vowel under the same consonant is called a *chataf sheva*. The *sheva* can be combined with a *patach* (ֲ), or a *kametz* (ֳ), or a *segol* (ֱ), and these forms will only appear under guttural letters and ר.

Since a guttural or a ר with a *sheva* would produce a weak sound, the vowel is added to strengthen the pronounced sound. The *chataf sheva* will follow the appropriate rules of the *sheva* that would have appeared under the letter without the vowel. The vowel in combination with the *sheva* will only provide a fuller sound, but not be considered a vowel in relation to the appropriate rules for long and short vowels and syllables.

A.   When a *chataf sheva* combines with a vowel at the beginning of a word, or inside a word after a long vowel, it functions as a *sheva na* (demanding to be read as part of the syllable with the consonant and vowel that follow it). This unique feature occurs when for example, you have a *chataf patach sheva* (ֲ), the *patach* sound is read, but the *patach* does not need to be closed by a *sheva nach* or a *dagesh chazak*, as it would need to if it was a regular vowel.

    a.   אֲשֶׁר

    b.   וּלְמוֹעֲדִים

    c.   חֲמִישִׁי

B.   The *chataf sheva* combines with the vowel under a guttural letter, after a letter with a short vowel. The *chataf sheva* closes the short vowel as a *sheva nach*, and doubles the reading of the guttural letter with the vowel, which is part of the *chataf sheva*. And, due to its nature as a *chataf sheva* the vowel does not need to be closed.

    a.   נַעֲשֶׂה

    b.   לְמַאֲכָל

    c.   הַחֲוִילָה

    d.   לַעֲבִיד

Chapter Two

Guttural & Dotted Letters

Four of the 23 letters are called gutturals.

THESE ARE:

א, ה, ח, ע

1. Gutturals will be a prime cause of change in the primary standard vowelling[1] patterns in all forms of words.

2. Guttural letters never take a *dagesh*[2] *chazak*. In addition to the four guttural letters, ר never takes a *dagesh*.

Regular Pattern	**With Guttural**

1. Normally a ה prefix has a *patach* (הַ), notice the guttural א follows the ה.	הָאֲנָשִׁים
2 As with 1 above, notice the ע follows the ה	הָעִיר
3. וַיְחַזִּיקוּ	וַיְחַזִּיקוּ
4. מָצָא, the א at the end of the word changes the standard צַ to צָ	מָצָא

If a vowelling and added letter pattern is not familiar to you, check the letter under which the irregular vowel appears, or the letter that follows the irregular vowel to see if it is a guttural letter.

End of Lesson 2

Don't miss your Self-Check Quiz!!

---

[1] Vowel: The sign of a sound, which appears under or right after any consonant.

[2] *Dagesh*: The name of the dot inside a letter.

Self-Check Quick Quiz

Questions

1. What kind of *sheva* is under ב in דְּבָרֵי?
2. What kind of *sheva* is under ת in פּוֹתְחִים?
3. What kind of *sheva* is under וְ in וְאָמֵן?
4. What kind of *chataf sheva* is under א in וְגוֹאֲלֵנוּ?
5. What kind of *sheva* is under ר in מְשָׁרְתִים?
6. What kind of *sheva* is under בּ in מְשַׁבְּחִים?
7. What kind of *sheva* is under בּ and ר of בְּיִרְאָה?
8. What is under שׁ in וְתִשְׁבָּחוֹת?
9. What kind of *chataf sheva* is under ה in בְּאַהֲבָה?
10. What kind of *sheva* is under ל in וּמִתְפַּלְלִים?
11. What *sheva* rule applies in תִּשְׁפְּטוּ?
12. What are the four primary guttural letters?
13. State two special features of a guttural letter.

Answers

1. *Sheva Nach.*
2. *Sheva Na.*
3. *Sheva Na.*
4. *Chataf Patach Sheva Na.*
5. *Sheva Na.*
6. This is a *Sheva Na* with a *dagesh chazak.*
7. The בּ is a *Sheva Na* and the ר is a *Sheva Nach.*
8. *Sheva Nach.*
9. *Chataf Patach Sheva Nach.*
10. *Sheva Na* pronounced as if the first ל has a *dagesh chazak* in it.
11. When two *Shevas* follow each other in a word, the first one is always a *sheva nach* following a short vowel and the second a *sheva na* opening a new syllable.
12. א, ה, ח, ע
13. Changes standard vowelling pattern, and does not take a *dagesh.*

Lesson 3

Rehov Beit Vegan 99, Yerushalayim 02.9920755
1091 River Ave., Lakewood NJ 08701 732.370.3344 fax 1.877.Pirchei (732.367.8168)

Chapter One

Syllables

Section One

There are three different ways that consonants and vowels can combine to form a syllable.

A. A consonant with a long vowel forms a syllable.

    a. בָּרָא

    b. לָאוֹר

    c. וְתֵרָא

B. A consonant with a short vowel, followed by a consonant with a *sheva nach* forms a syllable.

    a. יַבְדֵּל

    b. יִקְרָא

    c. מַבְדִּיל

C. A consonant with a short vowel, followed by a consonant with a long or short vowel, creates a demand for a *dagesh chazak* in the second consonant. (See Chapter 2, Section 2, B for the unique pronunciation rules of *dagesh chazak*) forms a syllable

    a. הַשָּׁמַיִם

    b. הַיַּבָּשָׁה (two *dagesh chazaks*)

    c. יַמִּים

Section Two

The syllables described in A-C above, are considered a single syllable, even when preceded by a consonant with a *sheva na* or a *chataf patach*, since the sound that the *sheva na* adds to the syllable is too weak to form a separate syllable. The following rules (D-F below) explain this principle.

D. A consonant with a *sheva na* followed by a letter with a long vowel forms a syllable.

    a. בְּרֵאשִׁית

    b. וְחֹשֶׁךְ

    c. פְּרִי

E. A consonant with a *sheva na*, followed by a consonant with a short vowel followed by a consonant with a *sheva nach* forms a syllable.

    a. לְהַבְדִּיל

    b. לְמֶמְשֶׁלֶת

    c. וְלִמְשֹׁל

F. A consonant with a *sheva na*, followed by a consonant with a short vowel, followed by a consonant with a *dagesh chazak* and its own vowel (long or short) forms a syllable.

    a. וְשִׁנַּנְתָּם

    b. בְּאַפָּיו

    c. לְבַדּוֹ

Summary

A long vowel under any consonant closes the syllable. A short vowel under a consonant must be closed by the following consonant having a *sheva nach*, or a *dagesh chazak*. The last syllables in a word, does not follow the rules for closing a syllable.

Chapter Two

The Dagesh (singular) and Dageshim (plural)

Section One

The *dagesh* is a dot in the center of a letter and can be placed in any letter except for the following:

א, ה, ח, ע, ר

There are two types of *dageshim*:

1. The *dagesh chazak* (**strong**)

2. The *dagesh kal* (**light**)

בגד כפת letters get either type of *dagesh* depending on circumstances, while all other letters besides ר ע ח ה[1] א can only get a *dagesh chazak*.

Section Two

1. **Dagesh Chazak (strong)**

   A. A letter that has its own vowel (long or short), which follows a letter with a short vowel, requires a *dagesh chazak* or when the letter that follows a letter with a short vowel has a *sheva na* under it, and a dagesh in that letter, this is a *dagesh chazak*.

        a. הַשָּׁמַיִם
        b. הַיּוֹם
        c. הַמָּאוֹר
        d. הַדְּבָרִים

   B. A *dagesh chazak* doubles the sound, but not the writing, of the letter in which it is placed. The first of the doubled letters has a *sheva nach* to close the previous letters short vowel, while the second of the doubled letters is read with its vowel or *sheva na*.

---

[1] The ה can get a *dagesh* at the end of a word. This is known as a *mapik* ה and will be clarified later.

a. הַשָּׁמַיִם = הַשְׁ־שָׁ־מַיְ־יִם

b. שִׁנַּנְתָּם = שִׁנְ־נַנ־תָּם

c. וְדִבַּרְתָּ = וְדִבְּ־בַּר־תָּ

2. **Dagesh Kal (light)**

The *dagesh kal* only appears in **BeGeD KeFeT** letters. Six of the 23 letters are known as **BeGeD KeFeT**.

THESE LETTERS ARE:

בְּגֶד—כְּפֶת

A. Each BeGeD KeFeT letter takes a *dagesh kal* whenever it begins a word, or whenever it is the first letter of a syllable following a *sheva nach* inside a word. The pronunciation varies according to the presence or absence of the *dagesh* and whether it is pronounced Ashkenazi, Sfardi or Temani. In this rule, inclusion or exclusion of the BeGeD KeFeT *dagesh* only alters pronunciation.

   a. בִּשְׁאוֹל

   b. פָּעֳלֵי

   c. תְּחִנָּתִי

B. When a BeGeD KeFeT letter follows א, ה, ו, י in a word or phrase (in the same sentence) and the BeGeD KeFeT is in a position that demands a *dagesh*, often no *dagesh* is placed in the BeGeD KeFeT letter. There are exceptions to this rule.

C. General examples:

   a. יָגַעְתִּי

   b. חַסְדֶּךָ

   c. תִּשְׁכָּחֵנוּ

   d. מִי כָמֹכָה   Dropping dagash kal.

   e. בְּדִבְרֵי תוֹרָה   Dropping dagash kal.

End Lesson 3

Don't miss your Self-Check Quiz ! !

Self-Check Quiz

Questions

1. How many syllables are there in תִּשְׁבַּע?
2. What type of *dagesh* is in תּ of תִּשְׁמֹר?
3. What type of *dagesh* is in שּׁ of מִשֶּׁבֶת?
4. What are the syllables of וְנֶאֱמַר?
5. What is the rule for a syllable?
6. How many syllables are there in אָנֹכִי?
7. What type of *dagesh* is in the תּ of בְּשִׁבְתְּךָ?
8. What type of *dagesh* is in the initial בּ?
9. How many syllables are there in לְטֹטָפֹת?
10. What type of *dagesh* is in the first and second בּ of בַּבֹּקֶר?
11. What type of *dagesh* is in מּ of סַמִּים?
12. What type of *dagesh* is in פּ of הַכִּפֻּרִים?
13. What type of *dagesh* is in תֶּ of שֶׁתֶּהֱא?
    And what is the *sheva* under the תֶּ?

Answers

1. תֵּשׁ-שָׁ-בַע.
2. *Dagesh kal.*
3. *Chazak.*
4. וְנֶא-אֱמַר.
5. Any group of letters with one long or short vowel.
6. אָ-נֹ-כִי.
7. *Dagesh kal.*
8. *Dagesh kal.*
9. לְטֹ-טָ-פֹת.
10. First בּ is *dagesh kal,* second בּ is *dagesh chazak*
11. *Chazak.*
12. *Dagesh chazak.*
13. *Dagesh chazak* and *sheva na.*

Lesson 4

Lesson

4

Verbal Lesson Inside Text Reading Practice

Exercise One: First Paragraph of Shemoheh Esrei — Amidah

This is a workbook. Therefore, if you want to fully benefit from the teachings within, you must also do the exercises. Even those who have prayed every day may not be enunciating their prayers properly. So, take your time and read the prayers slowly, focusing on the correct pronunciation. Do this with a friend.

כִּי שֵׁם ה' אֶקְרָא, הָבוּ גֹדֶל לֵאלֹהֵינוּ
אֲדֹנָי שְׂפָתַי תִּפְתָּח, וּפִי יַגִּיד תְּהִלָּתֶךָ

בָּרוּךְ אַתָּה יי אֱלֹהֵינוּ וֵאלֹהֵי אֲבוֹתֵינוּ, אֱלֹהֵי אַבְרָהָם אֱלֹהֵי יִצְחָק,

וֵאלֹהֵי יַעֲקֹב, הָאֵל הַגָּדוֹל הַגִּבּוֹר וְהַנּוֹרָא, אֵל עֶלְיוֹן, גּוֹמֵל חֲסָדִים

טוֹבִים וְקוֹנֵה הַכֹּל, וְזוֹכֵר חַסְדֵי אָבוֹת, וּמֵבִיא גוֹאֵל לִבְנֵי בְנֵיהֶם, לְמַעַן

שְׁמוֹ בְּאַהֲבָה. מֶלֶךְ עוֹזֵר וּמוֹשִׁיעַ וּמָגֵן. בָּרוּךְ אַתָּה יי, מָגֵן אַבְרָהָם.

When I call out the Name of Hashem, ascribe greatness to our G-d
My L-rd, open my lips, that my mouth may declare Your praise.

Blessed are you, Hashem, our G-d and the G-d of our forefathers, G-d of Abraham,
G-d of Isaac, and G-d of Jacob; the great, mighty, and awesome G-d, the supreme
G-d, Who bestows beneficial kindness and creates everything, Who recalls the
kindnesses of the Patriarchs and brings a Redeemer to their children's children, for His
Name's sake, with love. O King, Helper, Savior, and Shield. Blessed are You, Hashem
shield of Abraham.

Exercise Two: First Paragraph of the Grace after Meals

Let's now practice with another common prayer that people often rush though, *birchas hamazon*. Read each word as if you are reading it for the first time. You will experience a deep level of *davakus* (closeness to Hashem) as you say these words in the same way that the Holy Language is spoken in the Heavens.

בָּרוּךְ אַתָּה יי אֱלֹהֵינוּ מֶלֶךְ הָעוֹלָם, הַזָּן אֶת הָעוֹלָם כֻּלּוֹ, בְּטוּבוֹת בְּחֵן בְּחֶסֶד וּבְרַחֲמִים, הוּא נֹתֵן לֶחֶם לְכָל בָּשָׂר, כִּי לְעוֹלָם חַסְדּוֹ. וּבְטוּבוֹ הַגָּדוֹל, תָּמִיד לֹא חָסַר לָנוּ, וְאַל יֶחְסַר לָנוּ מָזוֹן לְעוֹלָם וָעֶד. בַּעֲבוּר שְׁמוֹ הַגָּדוֹל, כִּי הוּא אֵל זָן וּמְפַרְנֵס לַכֹּל וּמֵטִיב לַכֹּל, וּמֵכִין מָזוֹן לְכָל בְּרִיּוֹתָיו אֲשֶׁר בָּרָא. בָּרוּךְ אַתָּה יי, הַזָּן אֶת הַכֹּל.

Blessed are You Hashem, our G-d, King of the universe, Who nourishes the entire world in His goodness — with grace, with kindness, and with mercy. He gives nourishment to all flesh, for His kindness is eternal. And through His great goodness, we have never lacked, and may we never lack, nourishment for all eternity. For the sake of His great Name, because He is G-d Who nourishes and sustains all, and benefits all, and He prepares food for all of His creatures, which He has created. Blessed are You, Hashem, Who nourishes all.

Summary

You are using this book because Hebrew is not your mother tongue. However, even if you are fluent in speaking Hebrew this doesn't mean that you are pronouncing every word correctly. Many people say their prayers so fast that they have become habitual in their mispronunciation due to their need for speed. We all would be better off if we listen to our own prayers and seek to correct our mistakes. In this way we will come to understand their true meaning and elevate our heartfelt supplications. These shiurim are directed to help you achieve your goal of conscious and exact reading.

End of Lesson 4

Homework: Say the *Amida* and *Birchas Hamazon* slowly.
Focus on proper pronunciation.

Lesson 5

Rehov Beit Vegan 99, Yerushalayim 02.9920755

1091 River Ave., Lakewood NJ 08701 732.370.3344 fax 1.877.Pirchei (732.367.8168)

Lesson 5

Chapter One

Nouns

Definition

A **noun** is a word which names and identifies a person, place, thing, idea, or concept. Nouns can occur in the following four forms.

Masculine Singular	יֶלֶד (boy)	דּוֹד (uncle)
Masculine Plural	יְלָדִים (boys)	דּוֹדִים (uncles)
Feminine Singular	יַלְדָּה (girl)	דּוֹדָה (aunt)
Feminine Plural	יְלָדוֹת (girls)	דּוֹדוֹת (aunts)

There is no **neuter** in Hebrew. All nouns, verbs and adjectives must be either masculine or feminine. Some nouns (ex. דוד, ילד) can be expressed in both masculine and feminine forms based on a common root, while other nouns are either masculine or feminine and have a singular and plural form.

Masculine Singular	מָחוֹג (radius)	
Masculine Plural	מְחוֹגִים (radii)	
Feminine Singular	נִיחָה (rest)	
Feminine Plural	נִיחוֹת (rests)	

Section One: Gender Identification

A. Feminine Singular (נקבה)

If a noun ends in Xָה, Xַת, or XַXֶת in the singular form, it is feminine (נקבה) (with the exception of לַיְלָה).

Note: Xַת is always an indicator of the feminine noun in construct form; see Section I D.

    a.   הָאֲדָמָה

    b.   הָאִשָּׁה

    c.   הַבְּהֵמָה

    d.   מְדַבֶּרֶת

    e.   נְטִילַת (construct noun for feminine singular)

---

* X Represents any root letter

B. Masculine Singular (זכר)

If the root letters of a noun do not end in חָֽה, חָת, or חֶֽחָת, then the noun is masculine singular in the overwhelming majority of cases (except for those listed in Section Two A, B and C.)

    a.   רָקִיעַ

    b.   הָאָדָם

    c.   לְעָפָר

C. Feminine Plural

Feminine plural nouns end in אֹות.

    a.   סֻכֹּות

    b.   מִבְּכֹורֹות

    c.   וַאֲחֹות

D. Masculine Plural

Masculine plural nouns end in חִים.

    a.   הַכֹּוכָבִים

    b.   בָּנִים

    c.   הַשָּׁמַיִם

Section Two: Determining The Gender of a Noun

To determine the gender of a noun, examine its singular form and follow the guidelines expressed in Gender Identification. There are many more irregular forms of nouns in the plural than in the singular (far too many for a comprehensive list). Nevertheless, an overwhelming majority of plural nouns are true to form and gender.

Additionally, if any noun is followed by one or more adjectives, the adjective(s) are always true to the actual gender of the noun. (See Lesson 6, chapter two—Adjectives).

A. **Countries and cities** are usually feminine in gender, although, most of them are in masculine form (not exhaustive list).

    a.   אֶרֶץ

    b.   עִיר

    c.   יִשְׂרָאֵל

    d.   יְרֹשָׁלַיִם

    e.   יָוָן

    f.   רֹומָא

B. **Paired parts of the body** are feminine (and thus take feminine adjectives) even though almost all paired parts of the body are in masculine form (in both singular and plural).

a. (אָזְנַיִם) אֹזֶן

b. (יָדַיִם) יָד

c. (רַגְלַיִם) רֶגֶל

d. (עֵינַיִם) עַיִן

e. (שְׁנַיִם) שֵׁן

C. **There are a limited number of nouns, which are feminine, but do not have the typical feminine suffixes** (הX, תX, or תXX) in the singular. Here are most of these nouns.

		Singular	**Plural**	**Dual**
a.	Stone	אֶבֶן	אֲבָנִים	
b.	Fire	אֵשׁ	אִשִּׁים	
c.	Well	בְּאֵר	בְּאֵרוֹת	
d.	Stomach	בֶּטֶן	בְּטָנִים	
e.	Vine	גֶּפֶן	גְּפָנִים	
f.	Fence	גָּדֵר	גְּדֵרוֹת	
g.	Granary	גֹּרֶן	גְּרָנוֹת	
h.	Sword	חֶרֶב	חֲרָבוֹת	
i.	Courtyard	חָצֵר	חֲצֵרוֹת	
j.	Wedge	יָתֵד	יְתֵדוֹת	
k.	Cup	כּוֹס	כּוֹסוֹת	
l.	Spoon	כַּף	כַּפּוֹת	
m.	Tongue	לָשׁוֹן	לְשׁוֹנוֹת	
n.	Needle	מַחַט	מְחָטִים	
o.	Shoe	נַעַל	נְעָלִים	נַעֲלַיִם
p.	Soul	נֶפֶשׁ	נְפָשׁוֹת	
q.	Time	פַּעַם	פְּעָמִים	פַּעֲמַיִם
r.	Bird	צִפּוֹר	צִפֳּרִים	

Section Three: Definitiveness

All nouns in their simple form are indefinite (ex. *a book*). To form the definite noun from the indefinite noun, we add the definite article indicator letter 'ה' before the noun in its indefinite form.

a. הַכּוֹכָבִים
b. הַמְּאוֹרֹת
c. הַשָּׁנִים

When the initial root letter of the noun is a guttural ר, ע, or א, then often the definite prefix letter 'ה' will be vowelled with a *kametz* (ָ), rather than with a *patach* (ַ).

a. הָאָדָם
b. הָאִשָּׁה
c. וְהָאָרֶץ

The definite prefix letter 'ה' may be vocalized with a *segol* (ֶ), when the first root letter is ה, ח, or ע.

a. הֶחָבֵר
b. הֶעָרִים

When the definite noun has a prepositional prefix such as מ, ל, כ, or ב, along with the definitive 'ה', the 'ה' drops and the prepositional prefix takes the vowel of the 'ה', (either a *patach* (ַ) or a *kametz* (ָ)).

a. בַּגְּפָנִים = בְּ-הַגְּפָנִים
b. לָרָקִיעַ = לְ-הָרָקִיעַ
c. בַּיּוֹם = בְּ-הַיּוֹם

Special Note:
An interrogative sentence (question) may be introduced by the particle ה, with a *chataf patach* (הֲ).

Section Four: Dual Endings

In addition to singular and plural forms, there are Hebrew words that may be expressed in what is known as *dual form* or *dual ending*. This form exclusively indicates a pair of objects. Dual endings are commonly used with:

	Singular	**Plural**	**Dual**
Paired parts of the body (ex. Hands, feet)	יָד (hand)	יָדִים (hands)	יָדַיִם (two hands)
Items normally dealt with in pairs (ex. Shoes)	נַעַל (shoe)	נַעֲלוֹת (shoes)	נַעֲלַיִם (two shoes)
Units of time or count	יוֹם (day)	יָמִים (days)	יוֹמַיִם (two days)
	שָׁנָה (year)	שָׁנִים (years)	שְׁנָתַיִם (two years)

Special Note:

The *dual form* ending is identical for both masculine and feminine nouns.

End of Lesson 5

Homework: Review the *krias shema*. This time try to identify the nouns.

Lesson 6

Chapter One

Nouns (Continued)

Definition: The Construct Case (סמיכות *smichus***)**

When two nouns are linked together to create a single idea, the first of the two nouns carries the additional meaning של (*of*). The first of the two nouns is referred to as the *construct noun*.

When an unaccompanied noun is joined to another noun it forms the construct case. Example: *mountains* and *gold* in the construct become *mountains of gold*. The construct noun often undergoes a change when the implied של is added. These changes are dropping or changing letters and/or changing the vowelling patterns from the un-constructed noun form.

The **feminine singular** and **masculine plural** nouns change substantially when joined in construct form, when they are the construct nouns.

The masculine singular and feminine plural nouns when constructed may exhibit only slight changes.

The construct noun and the noun it is connected to when using של˙ do not have to agree in gender and number, but they must agree in definitiveness. With the rule being if the second noun of the construct is definite the entire construct is definite.

A. **Masculine singular nouns:**

The masculine singular noun does not change substantially when constructed.

אִישׁ שֶׁל חֶסֶד becomes אִישׁ חֶסֶד (man of kindness).

Below are some masculine singular construct nouns from the Torah.

a. רוּחַ אֱלֹקִים   The spirit of G-d
b. וְעֵץ הַחַיִּים   And the tree of life
c. עוֹף הַשָּׁמַיִם   The bird of the heavens

---

* The של (*of*) is implied, not written.

B. **Masculine plural nouns:**

Regular masculine plural nouns end in אִים, when constructed the מ drops and the י is now the final letter of the construct word. The letter preceding the final *yud* (יֹ) must have the vowel *tzarah* (ּ), under it.

חֲסָדִי אָבֹות becomes חֲסָדִים שֶׁל אָבֹות (kindness of the fathers).

Below are some masculine plural construct nouns from the Torah.

a. עַל פְּנֵי תְּהֹום   On the faces of the void
b. יֹדְעֵי טֹוב וָרָע   Knowers of good and bad
c. אַנְשֵׁי הַשֵּׁם   The men of renown

C. **Feminine singular nouns:**

Regular feminine singular nouns almost always end in אָה. However, when these nouns construct the אָ becomes אַ followed with a parallel change in the final letter from ה to the constructed ת.

נְטִילַת יָדַיִם becomes נְטִילָה שֶׁל יָדַיִם (washing of hands).

Below are some feminine singular construct nouns from the Torah.

a. נִשְׁמַת חַיִּים   Soul of life
b. חַיַּת הַשָּׂדֶה   The beast of the field

D. **Feminine plural nouns:**

The feminine plural noun does not change substantially when constructed. In both, construct and regular, the suffix is אֹות, slight vowelling changes might occur.

מְזוּזֹות בֵּיתְךָ becomes מְזוּזֹות שֶׁל בַּיִת שֶׁלְךָ

(*mezuzas* of your house)

Below are some feminine plural construct nouns from the Torah.

a. תֹּולְדֹות הַשָּׁמַיִם   The generations of the heavens
b. תֹּולְדֹות נֹחַ   The generations of Noah
c. מִשְׁפְּחֹות בְּנֵי נֹחַ   The families of the sons of Noah

E. **Construct nouns** are definite when the second part of the construct set is definite. There are three ways that the second noun of the construct set becomes definite to make the entire construct definite.

a. If the second noun has been made into a definite noun through the addition of the definitive prefix 'ה', the entire construct becomes definite.

וְעֵץ הַחַיִּים — And **the** tree of life

b. If the second noun of the construct is a definite noun (ex. Levy, Jerusalem, etc) then, the entire construct becomes definite.

תּוֹלְדוֹת נֹחַ — **The** generations of Noah

c. If the second noun of the construct has a possessive pronoun ending then, the entire construct becomes definite.

מַחְשְׁבוֹת לִבּוֹ — **The** thoughts of his heart

Chapter Two

Adjectives

Definition:

An **adjective** defines how or what of the noun it modifies, or it in some way qualifies or limits the noun. In *English* the adjective precedes the noun it qualifies; In *Hebrew* the adjective follows the noun it qualifies.

A. The noun and its adjective must agree in gender, number and definitiveness in translation, but not necessarily in form.

This	year		הַשָּׁנָה הַזֹּאת
adj.	*noun*		*adj.* *noun*

The four adjective endings are identical to the four noun endings, but unlike nouns adjectives always come in four forms. Adjectives are always true to the true gender and form of the nouns they qualify, even if the actual nouns have irregular endings.

A good student (m, s)	תַּלְמִיד טוֹב
A good student (f, s)	תַּלְמִידָה טוֹבָה
Good students (m, pl)	תַּלְמִידִים טוֹבִים
Good students (f, pl)	תַּלְמִידוֹת טוֹבוֹת
The good student (m, s)	הַתַּלְמִיד הַטּוֹב
The good student (f, s)	הַתַּלְמִידָה הַטּוֹבָה
The good students (m, pl)	הַתַּלְמִידִים הַטּוֹבִים
The good students (f, pl)	הַתַּלְמִידוֹת הַטּוֹבוֹת

The four adjective forms are:

			good	old (people)	big, great
a.	Masculine singular	×××	טוֹב	זָקֵן	גָּדוֹל
b.	Masculine plural	אִים	טוֹבִים	זְקֵנִים	גְּדוֹלִים
c.	Feminine singular	×××ָה	טוֹבָה	זְקֵנָה	גְּדוֹלָה
d.	Feminine plural	×××וֹת	טוֹבוֹת	זְקֵנוֹת	גְּדוֹלוֹת

B. When a noun that does not reflect its true gender is qualified by an adjective, the adjective is always true to form and gender. (The adjective will not follow the irregular noun form.)

    a.   הַלַּיְלָה הַזֶּה
    b.   וְהָעִיר הַגְּדוֹלָה
    c.   הַמְּאוֹרוֹת הַגְּדוֹלִים
    d.   אֲבָנִים גְּדֹלוֹת

C. Adjectives must parallel definite nouns and always have the definitive prefix ה when modifying a definite noun.

    a.   הֶהָרִים הַגְּבֹהִים
    b.   הַמַּסֹּת הַגְּדֹלוֹת
    c.   הַמְּאוֹרוֹת הַגְּדוֹלִים

D. Adjective Construct combinations.

תַּלְמִיד טוֹב	Masculine singular, noun and adjective.	A good student
הַתַּלְמִיד הַטּוֹב	Definite masculine singular, noun and adjective.	The good student
הַתַּלְמִיד טוֹב	Definite masculine singular, noun with a direct object.	The student is good
תַּלְמִיד הַטּוֹב	Definite construct noun.	**The** student of the good
תַּלְמִיד שֶׁל הַטּוֹב	Non-construct noun.	**A** student of the good

End of Lesson 6

Lesson 7

Rehov Beit Vegan 99, Yerushalayim 02.9920755

1091 River Ave., Lakewood NJ 08701 732.370.3344 fax 1.877.Pirchei (732.367.8168)

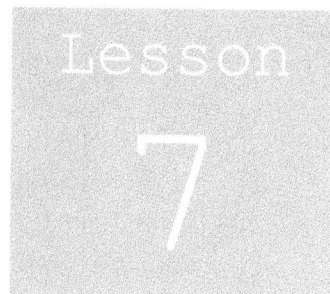

Chapter One

Pronouns

Definition:
A Pronoun is a specific word used to replace any form of a noun.

Section One: Subject Pronouns

Subject pronouns replace specific subject nouns of the sentence. This form is **only** used in place of the noun that is the subject of the sentence.

A. There is no expression of the neuter in Hebrew.

B. In the first person singular 'I' (אֲנִי), and the first person plural 'We' (אנחנו) there is one pronoun that functions equally in both masculine and feminine expressions.

C. In the second and third person there are unique pronouns for masculine and feminine expressions.

Singular

אֲנִי, אָנֹכִי	I (m/f)	First person
אַתָּה	You (m)	Second person
אַתְּ	You (f)	Second person
הוּא	He, it (m)	Third person
הִיא	She, it (f)	Third person

Plural

אָנוּ, אֲנַחְנוּ	We (m/f)	First person
אַתֶּם	You (m)	Second person
אַתֶּן	You (f)	Second person
הֵם, הֵמָּה	They (m)	Third person
הֵן, הֵנָּה	They (f)	Third person

Section Two: Demonstrative Pronouns

Demonstrative pronouns call attention to specific items. They can function as subject pronouns, object pronouns and adjectives.

זֶה, הַזֶּה	This (m, s)
זֹאת, הַזֹּאת	This (f, s)
אֵלֶּה	These (m/f, pl)
הַהוּא	That (m, s)
הַהִיא	That (f, s)
הֵם, הָהֵם	Those (m/f, pl)
הֵן, הָהֵן	Those (f, pl)

When demonstrative pronouns function as an adjective after a general or specific noun, always have the definitive pronoun prefix 'ה'.

כָּל הַמִּצְוֹת הָאֵלֶּה
כַּיּוֹם הַהוּא
הַדְּבָרִים הָאֵלֶּה

When demonstrative pronouns function as a regular subject or an object pronoun (not qualifying the noun), they do not take the definitive pronoun prefix 'ה'.

זֹאת הָאָרֶץ
זֶה הַדֶּרֶךְ
אֵלֶּה לְחַיֵּי עוֹלָם

Section Three: Direct Object Pronouns

The direct object pronouns answer the question "Whom" or "What" of a transitive verb, and must directly follow the verb.

There must be no preposition between the verb and the direct object.

The direct object pronoun can be expressed as a complete word separate from the verb or as a single or double letter suffix joined directly to the verb.

Singular

אוֹתִי	or	אִי, נִי	Me (m/f)	First person
אוֹתְךָ	or	ךָ	You (m)	Second person
אוֹתָךְ	or	אָךְ	You (f)	Second person
אוֹתוֹ	ו, יָו, הוּ, נוּ or		Him (m)	Third person
אוֹתָהּ	or	אָהּ	Her (f)	Third person

Plural

אוֹתָנוּ	or נוּ	Us (m/f)	First person
אֶתְכֶם	or כֶם	You (m)	Second person
אֶתְכֶן	or כֶן	You (f)	Second person
אוֹתָם	or ם	Them (m)	Third person
אוֹתָן	or ן	Them (f)	Third person

When the direct object is a separate word it looks as follows:

אֶרְאֶה אוֹתְךָ   I will show **you**.

When the direct object is joined as a suffix to the verb, it looks as follows:

אַרְאֶךָּ   I will show **you**.

When the direct object is a separate word from the verb:

וּקְשַׁרְתֶּם **אֹתָם**	And you will bind **them**.
וּרְאִיתֶם **אֹתוֹ**	And you will see **him**.
הֵן גֵּרַשְׁתָּ **אֹתִי**	Behold you banished **me**.

When the direct object is joined directly to the verb:

וַיַעַבְדֻנִי	And they will serve **me**.
וַיִּתְקָעֵהוּ	And he hurled **it**
וְשִׁנַּנְתָּם	And you will teach **them**

Note: *When the direct object ending is added directly at the end of a verb, there are usually drastic vowelling pattern changes, making binyan identification more difficult.*

The direct object pronoun letters may be added at the end of a preposition or prepositional phrase to become the direct object of the preposition.

Below is some sample text with the prepositional word *With* (עם) and *With* (את), joined to a complete set of object pronouns.

Singular

אִתִּי	עִמִּי	With me (m/f)	First person
אִתְּךָ	עִמְּךָ	With you (m)	Second person
אִתָּךְ	עִמָּךְ	With you (f)	Second person
אִתּוֹ	עִמּוֹ	With him (m)	Third person
אִתָּהּ	עִמָּהּ	With her (f)	Third person

Plural

אִתָּנוּ	עִמָּנוּ	With us (m/f)	First person
אִתְּכֶם	עִמָּכֶם	With you (m)	Second person
אִתְּכֶן	עִמָּכֶן	With you (f)	Second person
אִתָּם	עִמָּהֶם	With them (m)	Third person
אִתָּן	עִמָּהֶן	With them (f)	Third person

Section Four: Possessive Pronouns

Possessive pronouns follow the noun as either a separate word or joined directly to the noun as a pronoun possessive suffix. The possessive pronoun qualifies ownership of the noun.

The letters of the pronoun possessive letter suffix are identical to the direct object preposition suffix.

Singular

דוֹדוֹת (Aunties)	דוֹדָה (Aunt)	דוֹדִים (Uncles)	דוֹד (Uncle)		
דוֹדוֹתַי	דוֹדָתִי	דוֹדַי	דוֹדִי	שֶׁלִּי	My
דוֹדוֹתֶיךָ	דוֹדָתְךָ	דוֹדֶיךָ	דוֹדְךָ	שֶׁלְּךָ	Your
דוֹדוֹתַיִךְ	דוֹדָתֵךְ	דוֹדַיִךְ	דוֹדֵךְ	שֶׁלָּךְ	Your
דוֹדוֹתָיו	דוֹדָתוֹ	דוֹדָיו	דוֹדוֹ	שֶׁלּוֹ	His
דוֹדוֹתֶיהָ	דוֹדָתָהּ	דוֹדֶיהָ	דוֹדָהּ	שֶׁלָּהּ	Her

Plural

דוֹדוֹת (Aunties)	דוֹדָה (Aunt)	דוֹדִים (Uncles)	דוֹד (Uncle)		
דוֹדוֹתֵינוּ	דוֹדָתֵנוּ	דוֹדֵינוּ	דוֹדֵנוּ	שֶׁלָּנוּ	Our
דוֹדוֹתֵיכֶם	דוֹדַתְכֶם	דוֹדֵיכֶם	דוֹדְכֶם	שֶׁלָּכֶם	Your
דוֹדוֹתֵיכֶן	דוֹדַתְכֶן	דוֹדֵיכֶן	דוֹדְכֶן	שֶׁלָּכֶן	Your
דוֹדוֹתֵיהֶם	דוֹדָתָם	דוֹדֵיהֶם	דוֹדָם	שֶׁלָּהֶם	Their
דוֹדוֹתֵיהֶן	דוֹדָתָן	דוֹדֵיהֶן	דוֹדָן	שֶׁלָּהֶן	Their

Section Five: Direct Object, Object Preposition and Possessive Pronouns Suffixes

All of these letter endings are identical. The type of word they are joined to determines the function on these designated letters.

Me, mine (m/f)	אִי, נִי
Your, yours (m)	ךְ
Your, yours (f)	אֵךְ
Him, his (m)	וֹ, יָו, הוּ, נוּ
Her, hers (f)	אָהּ
Us, our (m/f)	נוּ
Yours (m, pl)	כֶם
Yours (f, pl)	כֶן
Them, theirs (m, pl)	ם
Them, theirs (f, pl)	ן

Mapik (הּ)

A *mapik* (הּ) only occurs at the end of a word. A regular ה may also occur at the end of a word without the dot.

When ה occurs at the end of a normal noun, it usually indicates a feminine singular noun[1]. When ה is at the end of a verb, it indicates the subject of the verb is in the feminine third person singular, past tense[2].

The ה at the end of a word becomes a *mapik* (הּ) when it performs one of three functions:

> **Note:** *A functioning* **mapik** *(הּ) does not always have a dot in the* ה, *and can still function like a* **mapik** *(הּ).*

A. At the end of a noun, it functions as the feminine third person singular, possessive pronoun (translation: *her*).

דּוֹדָה	Aunt	The regular ה indicates a feminine, singular noun.
דּוֹדָהּ	Her uncle	דּוֹד (uncle) plus the ה from שֶׁלָּהּ (her) and translates as '*her uncle*'. This is called the possessive pronoun *mapik* (הּ)

Examples

a.	כֹּחָהּ	Her/its strength
b.	רָחְבָּהּ	Her/its width
c.	קוֹמָתָהּ	Her/its height

---

[1] When a *mapik* (הּ) appears at the end of a noun it is the feminine third person possessive pronoun suffix.

[2] When a *mapik* (הּ) appears at the end of a verb it is the feminine third person singular direct object suffix.

At the end of a verb[3], it expresses the feminine third person singular, direct object of the verb.

שמרה	She guarded.
שמרה	He guarded her.

Examples

a.	לְעָבְדָהּ	To work it
b.	וּלְשָׁמְרָהּ	To guard her/it
c.	וַיְבִאֶהָ	He brought her/it

At the end of a preposition, it creates the feminine third person singular 'her' as the object of a preposition.

לָהּ	To her.
שֶׁלָּהּ	Hers (of her).

Examples

a.	לְמִינָהּ	To her kind
b.	לָהּ	To her/it
c.	בְּקִרְבָּהּ	At herself, inside her

---

[3] When a *mapik* (ה) is joined to a verb it may cause drastic variations in verb patterns, making *binyan* identification difficult.

Section Six: Chart

Prepositional, Adverbial and Other Phrases

3p, f, pl	3p, m, pl	2p, f, pl	2p, m, pl	1p, pl	3p, f, s	3p, m, s	2p, f, s	2p, m, s	1p, s		
אַיֵן	אַיָּם	אַיְּכֶן	אַיְּכֶם	אֵינוּ	אַיָּהּ	אַיּוֹ (אַיֵּהוּ)	אַיֵּךְ	אַיֵּךְ (אַיֶּכָה)	אַיִּי (אַיֵּנִי)	אֵי	where
אַחֲרֵיהֶן	אַחֲרֵיהֶם	אַחֲרֵיכֶן	אַחֲרֵיכֶם	אַחֲרֵנוּ	אַחֲרֶיהָ	אַחֲרָיו	אַחֲרַיִךְ	אַחֲרֶיךָ	אַחֲרַי	אַחַר	after
אֵינָן	אֵינָם	אֵינְכֶן	אֵינְכֶם	אֵינֶנּוּ	אֵינֶהָ	אֵינוֹ	אֵינֵךְ	אֵינְךָ	אֵינֶנִּי	אֵין	nothing
אֲלֵיהֶן	אֲלֵיהֶם	אֲלֵיכֶן	אֲלֵיכֶם	אֵלֵינוּ	אֵלֶיהָ	אֵלָיו	אֵלַיִךְ	אֵלֶיךָ	אֵלַי	אֶל	to, toward
אֶצְלָן	אֶצְלָם	אֶצְלְכֶן	אֶצְלְכֶם	אֶצְלֵנוּ	אֶצְלָהּ	אֶצְלוֹ	אֶצְלֵךְ	אֶצְלְךָ	אֶצְלִי	אֵצֶל	beside
אַשְׁרֵיהֶן	אַשְׁרֵיהֶם	אַשְׁרֵיכֶן	אַשְׁרֵיכֶם	אַשְׁרֵינוּ	אַשְׁרֶיהָ	אַשְׁרָיו	אַשְׁרַיִךְ	אַשְׁרֶיךָ	אַשְׁרֵי	אֲשֶׁר	who, whom
אוֹתָן	אוֹתָם	אֶתְכֶן	אֶתְכֶם	אוֹתָנוּ	אוֹתָהּ	אוֹתוֹ	אוֹתָךְ	אוֹתְךָ	אוֹתִי	אֵת (אֶת)	with
בָּהֶן	בָּהֶם	בְּכֶן	בְּכֶם	בָּנוּ	בָּהּ	בּוֹ	בָּךְ	בְּךָ	בִּי	בְּ	direct
בְּגִינָן	בְּגִינָם	בְּגִינְכֶן	בְּגִינְכֶם	בְּגִינֵנוּ	בְּגִינָהּ	בְּגִינוֹ	בְּגִינֵךְ	בְּגִינְךָ	בְּגִינִי	בְּגִין	with
בִּגְלָלָן	בִּגְלָלָם	בִּגְלַלְכֶן	בִּגְלַלְכֶם	בִּגְלָלֵנוּ	בִּגְלָלָהּ	בִּגְלָלוֹ	בִּגְלָלֵךְ	בִּגְלָלְךָ	בִּגְלָלִי	בִּגְלַל	for, in
בְּיָדֵיהֶן	בְּיָדֵיהֶם	בְּיָדֵיכֶן	בְּיָדֵיכֶם	בְּיָדֵינוּ	בְּיָדֶיהָ	בְּיָדָיו	בְּיָדֵךְ	בְּיָדֶיךָ	בְּיָדִי	בְּיָד	because
בֵּינֵיהֶן	בֵּינֵיהֶם	בֵּינֵיכֶן	בֵּינֵיכֶם	בֵּינֵינוּ	בֵּינָהּ	בֵּינוֹ	בֵּינֵךְ	בֵּינְךָ	בֵּינִי	בֵּין	for the
בִּלְתָּן	בִּלְתָּם	בִּלְתְּכֶן	בִּלְתְּכֶם	בִּלְתֵּנוּ	בִּלְתָּהּ	בִּלְתּוֹ	בִּלְתֵּךְ	בִּלְתְּךָ	בִּלְתִּי	בִּלְתִּי	between
בַּעֲבוּרָן	בַּעֲבוּרָם	בַּעֲבוּרְכֶן	בַּעֲבוּרְכֶם	בַּעֲבוּרֵנוּ	בַּעֲבוּרָהּ	בַּעֲבוּרוֹ	בַּעֲבוּרֵךְ	בַּעֲבוּרְךָ	בַּעֲבוּרִי	בַּעֲבוּר	not, except
בַּעֲדָן	בַּעֲדָם	בַּעַדְכֶן	בַּעַדְכֶם	בַּעֲדֵנוּ	בַּעֲדָהּ	בַּעֲדוֹ	בַּעֲדֵךְ	בַּעַדְךָ	בַּעֲדִי	בְּעַד	for the sake of
בְּעַצְמָן	בְּעַצְמָם	בְּעַצְמְכֶן	בְּעַצְמְכֶם	בְּעַצְמֵנוּ	בְּעַצְמָהּ	בְּעַצְמוֹ	בְּעַצְמֵךְ	בְּעַצְמְךָ	בְּעַצְמִי	בְּעֶצֶם	through
בִּפְנֵיהֶן	בִּפְנֵיהֶם	בִּפְנֵיכֶן	בִּפְנֵיכֶם	בְּפָנֵינוּ	בְּפָנֶיהָ	בְּפָנָיו	בְּפָנַיִךְ	בְּפָנֶיךָ	בְּפָנַי	בִּפְנֵי	in the selfsame
בִּשְׁבִילָן	בִּשְׁבִילָם	בִּשְׁבִילְכֶן	בִּשְׁבִילְכֶם	בִּשְׁבִילֵנוּ	בִּשְׁבִילָהּ	בִּשְׁבִילוֹ	בִּשְׁבִילֵךְ	בִּשְׁבִילְךָ	בִּשְׁבִילִי	בִּשְׁבִיל	in front of
בְּתוֹכָן	בְּתוֹכָם	בְּתוֹכְכֶן	בְּתוֹכְכֶם	בְּתוֹכֵנוּ	בְּתוֹכָהּ	בְּתוֹכוֹ	בְּתוֹכֵךְ	בְּתוֹכְךָ	בְּתוֹכִי	בְּתוֹךְ	for the sake of
דַּיָּן	דַּיָּם	דַּיְּכֶן	דַּיְּכֶם	דַּיֵּנוּ	דַּיָּהּ	דַּיּוֹ	דַּיֵּךְ	דַּיְּךָ (דַּיָּךְ)	דַּיִּי (דַּיֵּנִי)	דַּי (דֵּי)	inside
הִנָּן	הִנָּם	הִנְּכֶן	הִנְּכֶם	הִנֶּנּוּ (הִנֵּנוּ)	הִנָּהּ (הִנָּה)	הִנּוֹ (הִנְהוּ)	הִנֵּךְ	הִנְּךָ	הִנְנִי	הִנֵּה	enough
הֲרֵי הֵן	הֲרֵי הֵם	הֲרֵי אַתֶּן	הֲרֵי אַתֶּם	הֲרֵינוּ	הֲרֵיהִי	הֲרֵיהוּ	הֲרֵי אַתְּ	הֲרֵי אַתָּה	הֲרֵינִי	הֲרֵי	behold
זוּלָתָן	זוּלָתָם	זוּלַתְכֶן	זוּלַתְכֶם	זוּלָתֵנוּ	זוּלָתָהּ	זוּלָתוֹ	זוּלָתֵךְ	זוּלָתְךָ	זוּלָתִי	זוּלַת	behold
יֶשְׁנָן	יֶשְׁנָם	יֶשְׁכֶן	יֶשְׁכֶם	יֶשְׁנָה	יֶשְׁנָהּ	יֶשְׁנוֹ	יֶשֵׁךְ	יֶשְׁךָ	יֶשְׁנִי	יֵשׁ	except
כְּמוֹהֶן	כְּמוֹהֶם	כְּמוֹכֶן	כְּמוֹכֶם	כָּמוֹנוּ	כָּמוֹהָ	כָּמוֹהוּ	כָּמוֹךְ	כָּמוֹךָ	כָּמוֹנִי	כְּמוֹ	there is
כְּמוֹתָן	כְּמוֹתָם	כְּמוֹתְכֶן	כְּמוֹתְכֶם	כְּמוֹתֵנוּ	כְּמוֹתָהּ	כְּמוֹתוֹ	כְּמוֹתֵךְ	כְּמוֹתְךָ	כְּמוֹתִי	כְּמוֹת	like, as
כֻּלָּן	כֻּלָּם	כֻּלְּכֶן	כֻּלְּכֶם	כֻּלָּנוּ	כֻּלָּהּ	כֻּלּוֹ	כֻּלֵּךְ	כֻּלְּךָ	כֻּלִּי	כָּל	as it is
לָהֶן	לָהֶם	לָכֶן	לָכֶם	לָנוּ	לָהּ	לוֹ	לָךְ	לְךָ	לִי	לְ	all
לְאַטָּן	לְאַטָּם	לְאַטְּכֶן	לְאַטְּכֶם	לְאַטֵּנוּ	לְאַטָּהּ	לְאַטּוֹ	לְאַטֵּךְ	לְאַטְּךָ	לְאַטִּי	לְאַט	to
לְבַדָּן	לְבַדָּם	לְבַדְּכֶן	לְבַדְּכֶם	לְבַדֵּנוּ	לְבַדָּהּ	לְבַדּוֹ	לְבַדֵּךְ	לְבַדְּךָ	לְבַדִּי	לְבַד	slowly
לְמַעֲנָן	לְמַעֲנָם	לְמַעַנְכֶן	לְמַעַנְכֶם	לְמַעֲנֵנוּ	לְמַעֲנָהּ	לְמַעֲנוֹ	לְמַעֲנֵךְ	לְמַעַנְךָ	לְמַעֲנִי	לְמַעַן	alone
לִפְנֵיהֶן	לִפְנֵיהֶם	לִפְנֵיכֶן	לִפְנֵיכֶם	לְפָנֵינוּ	לְפָנֶיהָ	לְפָנָיו	לְפָנַיִךְ	לְפָנֶיךָ	לְפָנַי	לִפְנֵי	in order
לִקְרָאתָן	לִקְרָאתָם	לִקְרַאתְכֶן	לִקְרַאתְכֶם	לִקְרָאתֵנוּ	לִקְרָאתָהּ	לִקְרָאתוֹ	לִקְרָאתֵךְ	לִקְרָאתְךָ	לִקְרָאתִי	לִקְרַאת	before
לְתוֹכָן	לְתוֹכָם	לְתוֹכְכֶן	לְתוֹכְכֶם	לְתוֹכֵנוּ	לְתוֹכָהּ	לְתוֹכוֹ	לְתוֹכֵךְ	לְתוֹכְךָ	לְתוֹכִי	לְתוֹךְ	toward
מֵהֶן	מֵהֶם	מִכֶּן	מִכֶּם	מִמֶּנּוּ	מִמֶּנָּה	מִמֶּנּוּ	מִמֵּךְ	מִמְּךָ	מִמֶּנִּי	מִן	into
מוּלָן	מוּלָם	מוּלְכֶן	מוּלְכֶם	מוּלֵנוּ	מוּלָהּ	מוּלוֹ	מוּלֵךְ	מוּלְךָ	מוּלִי	מוּל	from
מִפְּנֵיהֶן	מִפְּנֵיהֶם	מִפְּנֵיכֶן	מִפְּנֵיכֶם	מִפָּנֵינוּ	מִפָּנֶיהָ	מִפָּנָיו	מִפָּנַיִךְ	מִפָּנֶיךָ	מִפָּנַי	מִפְּנֵי	opposite
נֶגְדָּן	נֶגְדָּם	נֶגְדְּכֶן	נֶגְדְּכֶם	נֶגְדֵּנוּ	נֶגְדָּהּ	נֶגְדּוֹ	נֶגְדֵּךְ	נֶגְדְּךָ	נֶגְדִּי	נֶגֶד	because of
נָכְחָן	נָכְחָם	נָכְחֲכֶן	נָכְחֲכֶם	נָכְחֵנוּ	נָכְחָהּ	נָכְחוֹ	נָכְחֵךְ	נָכְחֲךָ	נָכְחִי	נֹכַח	against
סְבִיבֵיהֶן	סְבִיבֵיהֶם	סְבִיבֵיכֶן	סְבִיבֵיכֶם	סְבִיבֵינוּ	סְבִיבֶיהָ	סְבִיבָיו	סְבִיבֵךְ	סְבִיבְךָ	סְבִיבִי	סָבִיב	opposite
עֲדֵיהֶן	עֲדֵיהֶם	עֲדֵיכֶן	עֲדֵיכֶם	עָדֵינוּ	עָדֶיהָ	עָדָיו	עָדַיִךְ	עָדֶיךָ	עָדַי	עַד (עֲדֵי)	surround
עוֹדָן	עוֹדָם	עוֹדְכֶן	עוֹדְכֶם	עוֹדֵנוּ	עוֹדָהּ	עוֹדוֹ	עוֹדֵךְ	עוֹדְךָ	עוֹדִי	עוֹד	until
עֲלֵיהֶן	עֲלֵיהֶם	עֲלֵיכֶן	עֲלֵיכֶם	עָלֵינוּ	עָלֶיהָ	עָלָיו	עָלַיִךְ	עָלֶיךָ	עָלַי	עַל (עֲלֵי)	still
עַל-יָדָן	עַל-יָדָם	עַל-יֶדְכֶן	עַל-יֶדְכֶם	עַל-יָדֵנוּ	עַל-יָדָהּ	עַל-יָדוֹ	עַל-יָדֵךְ	עַל-יָדְךָ	עַל-יָדִי	עַל-יַד	on
עִמָּהֶן	עִמָּהֶם	עִמְּכֶן	עִמְּכֶם	עִמָּנוּ	עִמָּהּ	עִמּוֹ	עִמָּךְ	עִמְּךָ	עִמָּדִי (עִמִּי)	עִם	near,
שֶׁלָּהֶן	שֶׁלָּהֶם	שֶׁלָּכֶן	שֶׁלָּכֶם	שֶׁלָּנוּ	שֶׁלָּהּ	שֶׁלּוֹ	שֶׁלָּךְ	שֶׁלְּךָ	שֶׁלִּי	שֶׁל	with
תַּחְתֵּיהֶן	תַּחְתֵּיהֶם	תַּחְתֵּיכֶן	תַּחְתֵּיכֶם	תַּחְתֵּינוּ	תַּחְתֶּיהָ	תַּחְתָּיו	תַּחְתַּיִךְ	תַּחְתֶּיךָ	תַּחְתַּי	תַּחַת	underneath

End of Lesson 7

Lesson 8

Rehov Beit Vegan 99, Yerushalayim 02.9920755
1091 River Ave., Lakewood NJ 08701 732.370.3344 fax 1.877.Pirchei (732.367.8168)

Static Words

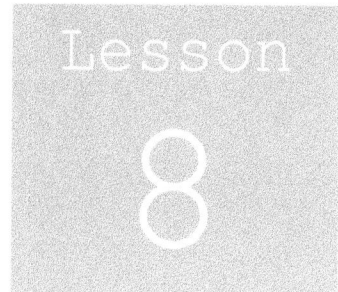

Lesson

8

Review Quiz

Question 1:
Identify the gender, number and definitiveness of these ten nouns:

	Translation	Masculine	Feminine	Singular	Plural	Definite	Indefinite
מְדַבֶּרֶת	A speaker						
הַשּׁוּלְחָנוֹת	The tables						
יַיִן	Wine						
נְטִילַת	Lifting/Washing						
הַיָּדַיִם	The hands						
עָרִים	Cities						
הַלֵּילוֹת	The nights						
חִלָּזוֹן	Snail						
הַגְּפָנִים	The vines						
הַמּוֹרָה	The teacher						

Question 2:
Identify the singular, plural and dual forms of these 3 words:

Singular	Translation	Plural	Dual
יוֹם	Day	_____	_____
אֶלֶף	One thousand	_____	_____
יָד	Hand	_____	_____

Question 3—Construct nouns:
Identify the following:

	Translation	Masc	Fem	Masc	Fem	Sing	Plural	Definite	Indefinite
יְמֵי נַעֲרֶהָ	The days of her youth								
בְּנֵי יִשְׂרָאֵל	The sons of Yisrael								
אֹהֶל מוֹעֵד	Tent of meeting								
מִשְׁפַּחַת גּוֹלד	The family of Gold								
מִכָּל הַבְּהֵמוֹת	From all the animals								
רֹאשׁ הָאַיִל	The head of the ram								
נַעֲרַת בֵּיתֶךָ	The girl of your house								
מִשְׁפָּחוֹת יְרוּשָׁלַיִם	The families of Jerusalem								

Question 4—Adjectives:
Match the adjective to the noun:

Noun		**Adjective**	
1)	הַמִּשְׁפָּחוֹת	a)	טוֹבָה
2)	אֶרֶץ	b)	הַגְּדוֹלִים
3)	יְלָדִים	c)	גָּדוֹל
4)	הַשׁוּלְחָנוֹת	d)	הַטּוֹבוֹת
5)	מַחְסָן	e)	גְּדוֹלִים
6)	הַמַּטְבֵּעַ	f)	הַטּוֹב

Question 5:
Match the pronoun with its definition:

Pronoun		**Definition**	
1)	הֵמָה	a)	Us
2)	אוֹתָנוּ	b)	These
3)	אֵלֶה	c)	They
4)	אֶתְכֶן	d)	Me
5)	הִיא	e)	She
6)	אוֹתִי	f)	You

Question 6:
Put these possessive pronoun endings, direct objects and object of preposition endings in proper order from me/mine ⇒ theirs:

Definition		**Endings**	
1)	Me/mine	a)	אָה
2)	You/yours	b)	ךָ
3)	His	c)	כֶם
4)	Hers	d)	הֶם
5)	Ours	e)	אָיו
6)	Yours (m)	f)	כֶן
7)	Yours (f)	g)	נוּ
8)	Theirs	h)	ִי

Question 7:
Identify the form with the meaning:

Meaning		**Form**	
1)	In the midst of us	a)	לָכֶן
2)	For you (f/pl)	b)	עִמָּה
3)	Against him	c)	אֶצְלִי
4)	With her	d)	בְּעַצְמֵנוּ
5)	Near me	e)	תַּחְתֵּיהֶם
6)	Under them	f)	נֶגְדוֹ

Question 8:
Using the following words for the constructs mentioned below:

1) עִיר   2) הָעִיר   3) הַקּוֹדֶשׁ   4) קְדוֹשָׁה   5) קוֹדֶשׁ

a) A holy city _____
b) The holy city _____
c) The city is holy _____
d) A city is holy _____
e) The city of holiness _____

Review Quiz Answers

Question 1:

	Translation	Masculine	Feminine	Singular	Plural	Definite	Indefinite
מְדַבֶּרֶת	A speaker		√	√			√
הַשׁוּלְחָנוֹת	The tables	√			√	√	
יַיִן	Wine	√		√			√
נְטִילַת	Lifting/Washing		√	√			√
הַיָדִים	The hands		√		√	√	
עָרִים	Cities		√		√		√
הַלֵּילוֹת	The nights	√			√	√	
חִלָּזוֹן	Snail	√		√			√
הַגְּפָנִים	The vines		√		√	√	
הַמוֹרָה	The teacher	√		√		√	

Question 2:

Singular	Translation	Plural	Dual
יוֹם	Day	יָמִים	יוֹמַיִם
אֶלֶף	One thousand	אֲלָפִים	אַלְפַּיִם
יָד	Hand	יָדִים	יָדַיִם

Question 3:

	Translation	Masc	Fem	Masc	Fem	Sing	Plural	Definite	Indefinite
יְמֵי נַעֲרָה	The days of her youth	√			√		√	√	
בְּנֵי יִשְׂרָאֵל	The sons of Yisrael	√		√			√	√	
אוֹהֶל מוֹעֵד	Tent of meeting	√		√		√			√
מִשְׁפַּחַת גוֹלד	The family of Gold		√	√		√		√	
מִכָּל הַבְּהֵמוֹת	From all the animals	√			√		√	√	
רֹאשׁ הָאַיִל	The head of the ram	√		√		√		√	
נַעֲרַת בֵּיתֶךָ	The girl of your house		√	√		√		√	
מִשְׁפְּחוֹת יְרוּשָׁלַיִם	The families of Jerusalem		√	√			√	√	

Question 4:

Noun		Adjective	
1)	הַמִשְׁפָּחוֹת	d)	הַטוֹבוֹת
2)	אֶרֶץ	a)	טוֹבָה
3)	יְלָדִים	e)	גְדוֹלִים
4)	הַשׁוּלְחָנוֹת	b)	הַגְדוֹלִים
5)	מַחְסָן	c)	גָדוֹל
6)	הַמַטְבֵּעַ	f)	הַטוֹב

Question 5:

Pronoun		Definition	
1)	הֵמָה	c)	They
2)	אוֹתָנוּ	a)	Us
3)	אֵלֶה	b)	These
4)	אֶתְכֶן	f)	You
5)	הִיא	e)	She
6)	אוֹתִי	d)	Me

Question 6:

Definition		Endings	
1)	Me/mine	h)	אִי
2)	You/yours	b)	ךָ
3)	His	e)	אָיו
4)	Hers	a)	אָה
5)	Ours	g)	נוּ
6)	Yours (m)	c)	כֶם
7)	Yours (f)	f)	כֶן
8)	Theirs	d)	הֶם

Question 7:

Meaning		Form	
1)	In the midst of us	d)	בְּעַצְמֵנוּ
2)	For you (f/pl)	a)	לָכֶן
3)	Against him	f)	נֶגְדוֹ
4)	With her	b)	עִמָה
5)	Near me	c)	אֶצְלִי
6)	Under them	e)	תַּחְתֵּיהֶם

Question 8:

a)	A holy city	עִיר קְדוֹשָׁה
b)	The holy city	הָעִיר הַקְּדוֹשָׁה
c)	The city is holy	הָעִיר קוֹדֶשׁ
d)	A city is holy	עִיר קוֹדֶשׁ
e)	The city of holiness	עִיר הַקְּדוֹשָׁה

End of lesson 8

LESSON 9

Rehov Beit Vegan 99, Yerushalayim 02.9920755
1091 River Ave., Lakewood NJ 08701 732.370.3344 fax 1.877.Pirchei (732.367.8168)

Chapter One

Lesson 9

The Shoresh (שרש)

A: Shoresh (שרש)

Three full letters in a definite order, without vowels (the same three letters in a different order have a different meaning). The *shoresh* (שרש) conveys a primal meaning that will influence all words incorporating the *shoresh* in its varied forms.

Examples

a.	ראה	Having to do with seeing or the eyes.
b.	אכל	Having to do with eating or food.
c.	כתב	Having to do with writing.
d.	ילד	Relating to children or birth.

B: Binyan

The *binyan* is an expression of the relationship of subject and predicate through the verb. There are seven *binyanim* reflecting the different facets of the שרש.

Binyan Chart

	REFLEXIVE[1]		CAUSATIVE	INTENSIVE	SIMPLE		
			מַפְעִיל	מְפַעֵל[2,3]	פּוֹעֵל	Present	A C T I V E
Present	מִתְפַּעֵל[1]		הִפְעִיל	פִּעֵל[2,3]	פָּעַל	Past	
Past	הִתְפַּעֵל[1]		יַפְעִיל	יְפַעֵל[2,3]	יִפְעֹל or יִפְעַל	Future	
Future	יִתְפַּעֵל[1]		(מְ) מָפְעָל	מְפֻעָל[3]	נִפְעָל	Present	P A S S I V E
			(הָ) הָפְעַל	פֻּעַל[2,3]	נִפְעַל	Past	
			(יְ) יָפְעַל	יְפֻעַל[2,3]	יִפָּעֵל	Future	

Notes 1,2 & 3 are found at top of pg. 48

- The direct object of the sentence in the פָּעַל *binyan* becomes the subject of the sentence in נִפְעַל *binyan*.
- The direct object of the sentence in the פָּעַל *binyan* becomes the subject of the sentence in פֻּעַל *binyan*.
- The direct object of the sentence in the הִפְעִיל *binyan* becomes the subject of the sentence in הֻפְעַל. *binyan*.
- The הִתְפַּעֵל the subject initiates action but doesn't control response in his own body or the one to whom the action is directed toward.

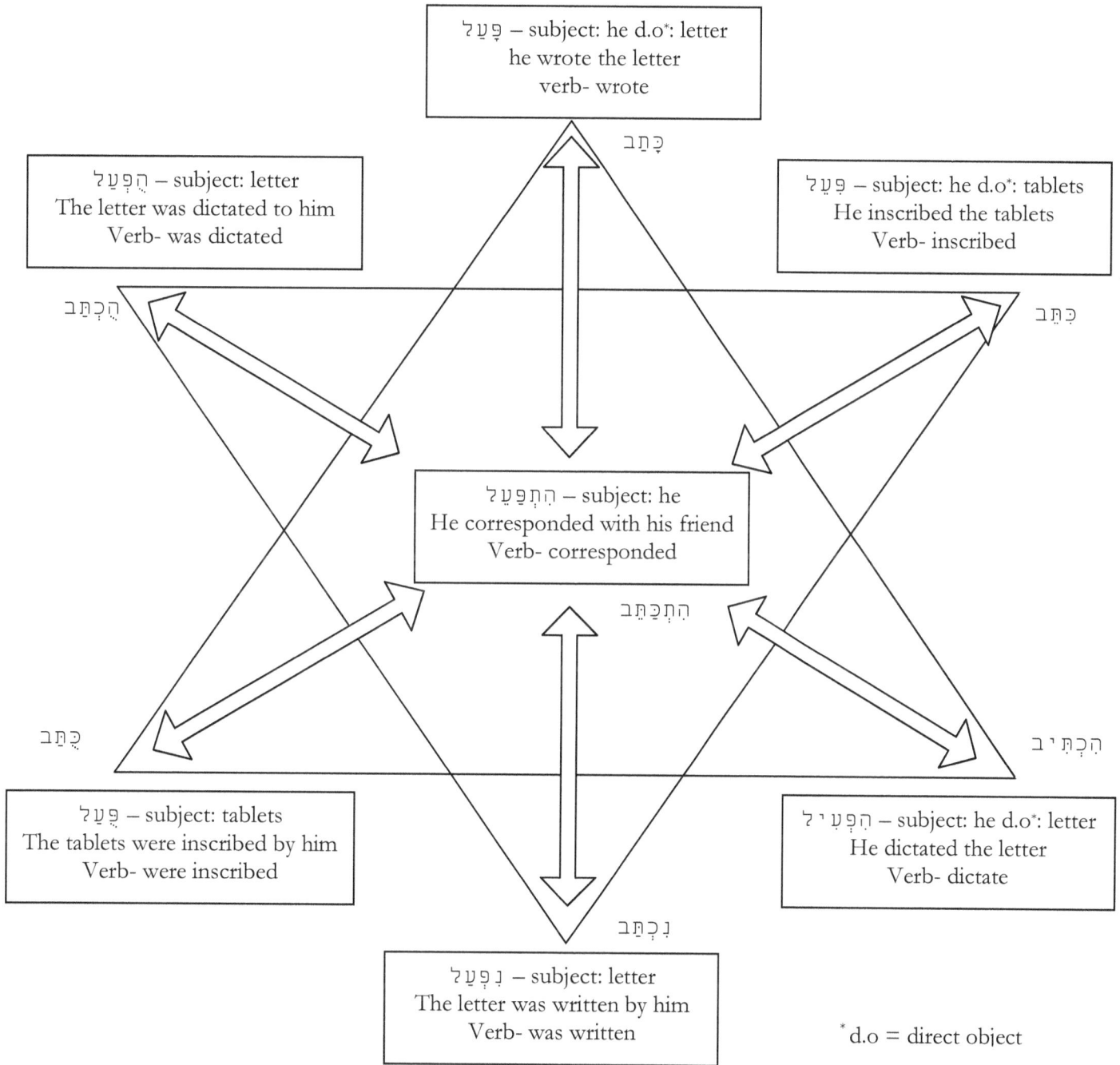

פָּעַל – subject: he d.o*: letter
he wrote the letter
verb- wrote

כָּתַב

הֻפְעַל – subject: letter
The letter was dictated to him
Verb- was dictated

הָכְתַב

פָּעַל – subject: he d.o*: tablets
He inscribed the tablets
Verb- inscribed

כָּתַב

הִתְפַּעֵל – subject: he
He corresponded with his friend
Verb- corresponded

הִתְכַּתֵב

פֻּעַל – subject: tablets
The tablets were inscribed by him
Verb- were inscribed

כֻּתַב

הִפְעִיל – subject: he d.o*: letter
He dictated the letter
Verb- dictate

הִכְתִּיב

נִפְעַל – subject: letter
The letter was written by him
Verb- was written

נִכְתַב

*d.o = direct object

These notes refer to Binyan chart pg. 46

(1)   Very important note: If the first root letter is שׂ, שׁ, or ס in the hit-phal *binyan*, the ת of the prefix יִת ,הִת ,מִת switches position with the root letter, as in הִשְׁתַּמְרוּ.

(2)   In the passive intensive *binyan* the actual voweling is מְפֹעָל – פֹּעַל – יְפֹעַל, since the guttural letter ע cannot receive a *dagesh chazak*.

(3)   The boxes so marked will need a *dagesh* in this ע position, if the middle root letter is not a guttural, as in דַּבֵּר.

Part 1: Binyan chart definitions

1. **Active:** The subject initiates the action of the verb.

2. **Passive:** The subject becomes the object of the action verb, or the direct object becomes the subject.

3. **Simple:** The subject either initiates, or receives the action of the verb in its basic/simplest primal expression.

4. **Intensive:** The translation of the verb (the verbal expression) increases in amount, intensity, duration, or emotion from the translation of the simple *binyan*.

5. **Causative:** The subject causes, or is caused to act. The initiator and actor are usually not the same person.

6. **Reflexive:** The subject acts on itself, resulting in a continuing involuntary response of the subjects initiated action, or to initiate a voluntary response from another in which the subject has no direct control.

Part Two: Binyan Identification

In potentiality and form, every root can be expressed through all the *binyanim*. Each unique *binyan* pattern reveals the operative factors found (above) in the Definition section. Each *binyan* has an absolutely unique vowelling pattern for easy identification, accompanied by standard patterns of extra, or changing, or dropping letters that precisely allow for absolute proper *binyan* identification. Additionally, each *binyan* can be expressed in the past, present and future tense. The *binyan* relation expression does not vary as the past, present and future find expression in a unique form or pattern. The primary *binyan* and tense identification patterns are found in the chart on page above, while person gender, number, tense indicators are revealed in the chart at the end of chapter 10.

Part Three: Binyan Nomenclature (classification)

The names of each of the *binyanim* (see the 7 shaded boxes in the chart above) incorporates the vowelling pattern and additional letter patterns that would/could be used with any three letter root. **The *binyan* name is always expressed in the masculine third person singular past tense using the root letter word "פעל".** There are only seven *binyan* names and seven *binyanim*, but there are 21 unique patterns to allow expression of the past, present and future in each *binyan*.

1. Active Simple—פָּעַל (*pa'al*)

The subject initiates and performs the action as expressed through the verb שרש letters in the most basic way.

כָּתַב	He wrote.
לָמַד	He Learned.

2. Active Intensive—פִּעֵל (*pi'el*)

The subject initiates and performs the action as expressed through the verb שרש letters in an intensified, longer, modified, or in any other mode where the tone of the action is an upgrade of the common expression. The *pi'el binyan* also functions as a causative form of the verb root, and translates similarly as the *hiph'il.*

כִּתֵּב	He inscribed.
לִמֵּד	He taught (i.e. He caused learning).

3. Active Causative—הִפְעִיל (*hiph'il*)

The subject initiates the action as expressed through the verb שרש letters. The subject never does the action, but causes another/others to do the action.

הִכְתִּיב	He dictated.

4. Reflective—הִתְפַּעֵל (*hispa'el*)

Usually has a side of active initiation and a side of passive receptivity, or involuntary action. It is a combination of the active and passive modalities.

הִתְכַּתֵּב	He corresponded. (i.e. He was not in control of the person he wrote to responding.)

5. **Passive Simple—נִפְעָל** (*niph'al*)

The subject receives the result of the simple action. A second definition is what was the direct object of the active transitive verbs, is now the subject of the statement.

נִכְתַּב   It was written.

6. **Passive Intensive—פֻּעַל** (*poo'al*)

The subject of the sentence receives the result of the intensified action. Here also the direct object of the active form is now the subject.

כֻּתַּב   It was inscribed.

7. **Passive Causative—הֻפְעָל** (*hooph'al*)

The subject is caused to do an action, which was initiated by someone or something other than the subject. Here also, the object of the causative word is now the subject.

הֻכְתַּב   It was dictated.

Letters as Prefix, Suffix, Infix...

Additionally there are other letter combinations and vowel patterns, which when attached to the *shoresh* letter indicate Tense, Gender, Number and Person (TGNP). Although a root letter may drop, vowels may change or letters may be added, there must always be a *binyan* and TGNP sign present in every verb.

VERB BINYAN DITTY:

פָּעַל–פִּעֵל–הִפְעִיל–הִתְפַּעֵל–נִפְעָל–פֻּעַל–
הֻפְעַל

Verb Binyan Ditty: הֻפְעַל
עִיל–הִתְפַּעֵל–נִפְעָל–פֻּעַל–
פָּעַל–פִּעֵל–הֻפ

- The פָּעַל *binyan* has a *kametz* under the first root letter. The פִּעֵל *binyan* has a short vowel, either a *patach* or a *hirik*, under the first root letter; and a full vowel under the second root letter with a *dagesh chazak* in it. The הִפְעִיל *binyan* has a ה prefix with a *hirik* under the ה. And the הִתְפַּעֵל has a הת prefix with a *hirik* under the ה and a *sheva nach* under the ת.

- In the passive forms the נִפְעַל *binyan* must have a נ prefix with a *hirik*. And the פֻּעַל *binyan* has a *kubutz* under the first root letter, a full vowel under the second root letter with a *dagesh chazak* in it. Finally in the past tense, the הֻפְעַל *binyan* must have a ה prefix with a *kubutz*, and a *sheva nach* under the first root letter.

- Five of the *binyanim* must have a מ prefix in the present tense; they are the Intensive Active and Passive, the Causative Active and Passive, and the Reflexive.

- The Intensive Present tense must have a מ prefix with a *sheva na*, followed by a root letter with a short vowel.

- If the short vowel is a *patach* or a *hirik*, it indicates the Intensive Active Present tense.

- If the short vowel under the first root letter is a *kubutz*, it indicates the Intensive Passive Present tense.

- If the מ prefix has a *patach* (and usually a י between the second and third root letters), it indicates the Causative Active, while the Causative Passive Present has a *kubutz* or *kametz* under the מ prefix.

- The הִת of the Reflexive in the past becomes מִת in the present.

- To form the future tense of the five *binyanim* that have a מ prefix in the present tense, drop the מ prefix and replace it with the appropriate future tense letter א, ת, י or נ and keep the vowels as they were in the present tense.

- The sign of the present tense in the פָּעַל *binyan* is a *holom* (וֹ) between the first and second root letters.

- The sign of the future tense of the פָּעַל *binyan* is the prefix א, ת, י or נ with a *hirik*, and a *sheva nach* under the first root letter.

- The sign of the present tense of the נִפְעַל *binyan* is a נ prefix with a *hirik*, a *sheva nach* under the first root letter, and a *kametz* under the second root letter. The future tense of the נִפְעַל *binyan* is unique as the prefix letter א, ת, י or נ must have a full vowel (long or short) and the first and second root letters must also have full vowels (long or short), with no *sheva* under the prefix letter or first two root letters.

- Only א, ת, י, נ, מ, ה may be prefix letters for verb roots.

End of Lesson 9

Rehov Beit Vegan 99, Yerushalayim 02.9920755
1091 River Ave., Lakewood NJ 08701 732.370.3344 fax 1.877.Pirchei (732.367.8168)

Chapter One

Unique Signs

Identifying Each Binyan in Every Tense

The following information is an explanation of the primary sign indicators that identify the three tenses of the seven *binyanim* of שלמים verbs (no gutturals, no dropping letters) in the seven *binyanim*.

General Rule:

The present tense of the verb in all the active *binyanim* can also serve as the noun form of the verb *shoresh*. In the passive forms נִפְעַל (passive simple), a special form פָּעוּל serves as the adjective according to some opinions, and the הֻפְעַל and פֻּעַל the present tense also serve as the adjective form of the *shoresh* .

Active Simple	Present tense	שׁוֹמֵר
פָּעַל – *pa'al*	There is a *holom* (וֹ) between the first and second letter of the *shoresh*: xxֹx.	עוֹבֵד רוֹכֵב
	Past tense There is a *kametz* (ָ) under the first letter of the *shoresh* and a *patach* (-) under the second letter of the *shoresh*: xxֲx.	שָׁמַר עָבַד רָכַב
	Future tense There is a *hirik* (.) under the prefix of the future tense and a *sheva* (:) under the first letter of the *shoresh*: xxxִF*	יִשְׁמֹר תִּזְכֹּר נִדְבַּק

---

* F = the prefix for the **F**uture tense.

Active Intensive פָּעֵל – *pi'el*	**Present tense** There is a *sheva* (׃) under the מ prefix, a short vowel under the first letter of the *shoresh,* either a *hirik* (.) or a *patach* (-), and a full vowel (i.e. not a *sheva*) and *dagesh chazak* in the middle letter of the *shoresh*: מְאַסֵּx.	מְדַבֵּר מְיַשֵּׁב מְצַוֶּה
	Past tense There is a short vowel, either a *hirik* (.) or a *patach* (-), under the first letter of the *shoresh,* and a full vowel under the middle letter, which takes a *dagesh*: xסֵּx or xסָּx or xסֶּx.	דִּבֵּר שִׁלֵּח סִכֵּן
	Future tense There is a *sheva* (׃) under the prefix of the future tense, with a short vowel under the first letter of the *shoresh*–either a *hirik* (.) or a *patach* (-), and a full vowel under the middle letter, which takes a *dagesh chazak*: xסַּxF. Vowelling is exactly the same as in the present tense.	יְדַבֵּר תְּשַׁלַּח נְסַכֵּן
Active Causative הִפְעִיל – *hiph'il*	**Present tense** There is a *patach* (-) under the מ prefix, a *sheva nach* (׃) under the first root letter and a י between the second and third letters of the *shoresh*: מַxxיx. There is no י in a root with ה as the last root letter.	מַקְצִיר מַשְׁאִיל מַנְחִיל יַעֲלֶה תַקְנֶה
	Past tense There is a *hirik* (.) under the ה prefix, a *sheva nach* (׃) under the first root letter and a י between the second and third letters of the *shoresh,* in the third person only (first and second person has no י): הִxxיx.	הִקְצִיר הִזְכִּיר הִשְׁאִיל הִזְכַּרְתְּ הִפְקַדְנוּ
	Future tense There is a *patach* (-) under the prefix of the future tense and a *sheva* (׃) under the first letter and a י between the second and third letters of the *shoresh*: xיxxF. There is no letter י in a root with a ה as the last root letter. Vowelling is exactly like the present tense.	יַקְצִיר תַזְכִּיר יַשְׁאִיל

Reflective הִתְפַּעֵל – *hispa'el*	**Present tense** There is a *hirik* (.) under the מ prefix, a *sheva* (־) under the ת of the מת prefix followed by the *shoresh* which, carries the same vowelling pattern as the corresponding פִּעֵל, past tense form: מתXXX (if not exact, than very similar to פִּעֵל form).	מִתְקַשֵּׁר מִתְנַפֵּל
	Past tense There is a *hirik* (.) under the ה and a *sheva* (־) under the ת of the הת prefix followed by the *shoresh* which, carries the same vowelling pattern as the corresponding פִּעֵל, past tense form: הִתXXX.	הִתְקַשֵּׁר הִתְיַשַּׁבְתֶּם
	Variations When the first root letter is a ז or צ there occurs a unique pattern. • If the first root letter is ז then the ת of the הת is replaced by a ד and becomes הד, and the ד switches with the root letter ז. הִזְדַּקֵּף ⇐ הדזקף ⇐ התזקף ⇐ זקף הִזְדָּרֵז ⇐ הדזרז ⇐ התזרז ⇐ זרז • When the first root letter is a צ the הת becomes הט, and the צ switches with the ט. הִצְטַדֵּק ⇐ הטצדק ⇐ התצדק ⇐ צדק **Note:** the same rule applies in the future and present tenses.	הִזְדַּקֵּף הִזְדָּרֵז הִצְטַדֵּק
	Future tense There is a *hirik* (.) under the future tense and a *sheva* (־) under the ת of the ית prefix followed by the *shoresh*, which carries the same vowelling pattern as the corresponding פִּעֵל, past tense form XXXיתֵ.	יִתְקַשֵּׁר נִתְיַשְּׁבוּ
Passive Simple נִפְעַל – *niph'al*	**Present tense** There is a *hirik* (.) under the נ prefix, a *sheva* (־) under the first letter of the *shoresh* and a *kametz* (ָ) under the middle root letter: נXXֶX.	נִשְׁמָר נִזְכָּרִים נִשְׁלָחוֹת
	Past tense Same as the Present tense with a *patach* (־) under the middle letter of the *shoresh*: נXXֶX.	נִשְׁמַר נִזְכַּרְתִּי נִשְׁלַחְתֶּן

	Future tense There is a future tense prefix with a full vowel followed by two full vowels under the first two letters of the *shoresh* (i.e. no sheva) This is unique: xxxF	יִשָּׁמֵר נִזְכֵּר תִּשָּׁאֲלִי
Passive Intensive פֻּעַל – *poo'al*	**Present tense** There is a *sheva* (ְ) under the מ prefix, a *kubutz* (ֻ) under the first letter of the *shoresh* and a full vowel under the middle letter of the *shoresh* which takes a *dagesh*: xΘΘx	מְכֻבָּד מְיֻסָּדוֹת
	Past tense There is a *kubutz* (ֻ) under the first letter of the *shoresh* and a and a full vowel under the middle letter of the *shoresh* which takes a *dagesh chazak*: xΘx	כֻּבַּד נֻטַּשְׁתִּי
	Future tense There is a *sheva* (ְ) under the prefix of the future tense with a *kubutz* (ֻ) under the first letter of the *shoresh* and a and a full vowel under the middle letter of the *shoresh* which takes a *dagesh chazak*: xΘxF. Exact pattern as the present tense.	יְסֻכַּן יְצֻמַּת יְהֻלְּלוּ
Passive Causative הֻפְעַל – *hooph'al*	**Present tense** There is a *kubutz* (ֻ) or a *kametz* (ָ) *katan* under the מ prefix, and a *sheva* (ְ) under the first letter of the *shoresh*: xxxמ.	מֻקְצָרִים מֻחְזָק מֻנְחָלוֹת
	Past tense There is a *kubutz* (ֻ) or a *kametz* (ָ) *katan* under the ה prefix, and a *sheva* (ְ) under the first letter of the *shoresh*: xxxהָ.	הֻקְצַר הָאֲכַלְתִּי
	Future tense There is a *kubutz* (ֻ) or a *kametz* (ָ) *katan* under the future tense prefix, and a *sheva* (ְ) under the first letter of the *shoresh*: xxxF. Exact pattern as the present tense.	תֻּקְצַרְנָה יֻבְטְחוּ

Chapter Two

Number, Person, Gender, Tense Chart

Number		Person	Gender	Past		Present		Future	
S I N G U L A R (s)	1	I	M	XXXתִּי	(1)	XXX, XXֹX	(4)	אXXX	(8)
		I	F	XXXתִּי	(1)	XXXָה, XXֶֶת	(5)	אXXX	(8)
	2	You	M	XXXתָּ		XXX, XXֹX	(4)	תXXX	(9)
		You	F	XXXתְּ		XXXָה, XXֶֶת	(5)	תXXXי	
	3	He	M	XXX		XXX, XXֹX	(4)	יXXX	
		She	F	XXXה		XXXָה, XXֶֶת	(5)	תXXX	(9)
P L U R A L (pl)	1	We	M	XXXנוּ	(2)	XXXים	(6)	נXXX	(10)
		We	F	XXXנוּ	(2)	XXXות	(7)	נXXX	(10)
	2	You	M	XXXתֶּם		XXXים	(6)	תXXXוּ	
		You	F	XXXתֶּן		XXXות	(7)	תXXXנָה	(11)
	3	They	M	XXXוּ	(3)	XXXים	(6)	יXXXוּ	
		They	F	XXXוּ	(3)	XXXות	(7)	תXXXנָה	(11)

Past Tense

(1)   Within each *binyan* 1p,m,s and 1p,f,s forms are identical in the Past Tense.

(2)   Within each *binyan* 1p,m,pl and 1p,f,pl forms are identical in the Past Tense.

(3)   Within each *binyan* 3p,m,pl and 3p,f,pl forms are identical in the Past Tense.

Present Tense

(4)   Within each *binyan* all *m,s* forms are identical in the Present Tense.

(5)   Within each *binyan* all *f,s* forms are identical in the Present Tense.

(6)   Within each *binyan* all *m,pl* forms are identical in the Present Tense.

(7)   Within each *binyan* all *f,pl* forms are identical in the Present Tense.

Future Tense	(8)	Within each *binyan* 1p,m,s and 1p,f,s forms are identical in the Future Tense.
	(9)	Within each *binyan* 2p,m,s and 3p,f,s forms are identical in the Future Tense.
	(10)	Within each *binyan* 1p,m,pl and 1p,f,pl forms are identical in the Future Tense.
	(11)	Within each *binyan* 2p,m,pl and 3p,f,pl forms are identical in the Future Tense.

| Past Tense | The above suffix endings NEVER change, regardless of Binyan or dropping letters. They are always present with the vowelling indicated, except at times when the direct object is attached at the end of the verb, at which time, although the letters must remain, the vowels change. |

| Future Tense | The letter indicators in the above chart are ALWAYS present in any future tense verb, regardless of *binyan* or dropping letters. However, the vowel under the prefix letter varies according to the first letter of the root and *binyan*. |

In addition to indicating Tense, the prefix and/or suffix (of a verb) indicate(s) Person, Number, and Gender. Please take note that in the Past and Future Tenses, the prefix and suffix come in 9 (not 12) forms due to the double Gender of the first person singular and plural, and third person plural. Unlike the Present Tense, which has only four forms with consistent endings in all *binyanim*, in the Past and Future Tenses each person (1, 2, 3) is unique in form. The Present Tense consists of only the following four forms *m,s*; *f,s*; *m,pl*; and *f,pl*. The noun or subject pronoun in a sentence in the Present Tense determines the definite Person and Gender of the verb. The forms of the Present Tense verb in all seven *binyanim* are described previously.

End of Lesson 10

Lesson 11

Rehov Beit Vegan 99, Yerushalayim 02.9920755
1091 River Ave., Lakewood NJ 08701 732.370.3344 fax 1.877.Pirchei (732.367.8168)

Regular Shoresh Binyan Test

Person	Number	Gender	Tense	Binyan	Shoresh	Word	Blessing
						תִּפְתַּח	1
						קוֹנֶה	1
						מְחַיֶּה	2
						מְקַיֵּם	2
						מַצְמִיחַ	2
						נְקַדֵּשׁ	3
						וְקָרָא	3
						יִמְלֹךְ	3
						נַקְדִּישׁ	3
						יְהַלְלוּ	3
						חוֹנֵן	4
						מְלַמֵּד	4
						חָטָאנוּ	6
						נִרְפָּא	8
						מְקַבֵּץ	9
						יִכָּרְתוּ	12
						מַכְנִיעַ	12
						דִּבַּרְתָּ	14
						תַּצְמִיחַ	15
						מַצְמִיחַ	15
						שׁוֹמֵעַ	16
						תֶּחֱזֶינָה	17
						מַחֲזִיר	17
						יִתְבָּרַךְ	18

Answers

Person	Number	Gender	Tense	Binyan	Shoresh	Word	Blessing
2 or 3	S	M / F	Future	פָּעַל	פ.ת.ח	תִּפְתַּח	1
1,2,3	S	M	Present	פָּעַל	ק.נ.ה	קוֹנֶה	1
1,2,3	S	M	Present	פָּעַל	ח.י.ה	מְחַיֶּה	2
1,2,3	S	M	Present	פָּעֵל	ק.י.ם	מְקַיֵּם	2
1,2,3	S	M	Present	הִפְעִיל	צ.מ.ח	מַצְמִיחַ	2
1	Pl	M / F	Future	פָּעֵל	ק.ד.ש	נְקַדֵּשׁ	3
3	S	M	Past	פָּעַל	ק.ר.א	וְקָרָא	3
3	S	M	Future	פָּעַל	מ.ל.ך	יִמְלֹךְ	3
1	Pl	M / F	Future	הִפְעִיל	ק.ד.ש	נַקְדִּישׁ	3
3	Pl	M	Future	פָּעֵל	ה.ל.ל	יְהַלְלוּ	3
1,2,3	S	M	Present	פָּעַל	ח.נ.ן	חוֹנֵן	4
1,2,3	S	M	Present	פָּעֵל	ל.מ.ד	מְלַמֵּד	4
1	Pl	M / F	Past	פָּעַל	ח.ט.א	חָטָאנוּ	6
1	Pl	M / F	Future	נִפְעַל	ר.פ.א	נֵרָפֵא	8
1,2,3	S	M	Present	פָּעֵל	ק.ב.ץ	מְקַבֵּץ	9
3	Pl	M	Future	נִפְעַל	כ.ר.ת	יִכָּרְתוּ	12
1,2,3	S	M	Present	הִפְעִיל	כ.נ.ע	מַכְנִיעַ	12
2	S	M	Past	פָּעַל	ד.ב.ר	דִּבַּרְתָּ	14
2 or 3	S	M / F	Future	הִפְעִיל	צ.מ.ח	תַּצְמִיחַ	15
1,2,3	S	M	Present	הִפְעִיל	צ.מ.ח	מַצְמִיחַ	15
1,2,3	S	M	Present	פָּעַל	ש.מ.ע	שׁוֹמֵעַ	16
2 or 3	Pl	F	Future	פָּעַל	ח.ז.ה	תֶּחֱזֶינָה	17
1,2,3	S	M	Present	הִפְעִיל	ח.ז.ר	מַחֲזִיר	17
3	S	M	Future	הִתְפַּעֵל	ב.ר.ך	יִתְבָּרֵךְ	18

End of Lesson 11

Lesson 12

Rehov Beit Vegan 99, Yerushalayim 02.9920755
1091 River Ave., Lakewood NJ 08701 732.370.3344 fax 1.877.Pirchei (732.367.8168)

Replacing or Dropping Letters

Six Important Letters

Six letters in Hebrew alphabet have the special quality of being replaced or being dropped from the *shoresh* in certain word forms regularly.

These letters are:

- א, נ, י   In the פ position (the position of the first *shoresh* letter).
- ו, י   In the ע position (the position of the second *shoresh* letter).
- ה   In the ל position (the position of the third *shoresh* letter).

ל	ע	פ
ה	ו	א
נ	י	נ
		י
		ל*

General Rule: When a prefix, infix, or suffix is applied to a *shoresh* adjacent to one of the above root letters, the prefix, infix, or suffix may cause one of these root letters to change or disappear completely. Even though these letters disappear, a sign remains in the word to alert us that one of the root letters has dropped. The circumstances under which letters actually drop and the signs left behind which indicate the drop are explained and illustrated below.

---

* Unusual form, like פ-נ

A. א-פ

The א physically drops from the *shoresh* only in the *pa'al binyan* in the first person singular of the future tense. The form calls for the prefix א, which would result in two אs at the beginning of the word. Instead the א of the root, in the first person only, drops, leaving only the א of the future tense (I will).

The *shoresh* אכל   ⇒   אֹכַל   I will eat

1. Sometimes the א in the פ position of the *shoresh* in the *pa'al*, future tense does not physically drop. However, it does drop in the sense that it takes no vowel, thus rendering it completely silent (i.e. it is dropped completely from pronunciation).

The *shoresh* אכל   ⇒   יֹאכַל   He will eat

  ⇒   תֹּאכַל   You will eat

  ⇒   יֹאכְלוּ   They will eat

Note: No vowel is associated with the א

2. Often the א in the פ position of the *shoresh* remains in all forms, including the first person singular, and it vowelling is doubled.

The *shoresh* אמר   ⇒   אֲאֵמֹר   I will say

The *shoresh* אמנ   ⇒   אֲאֵמֹן   I will trust

The *shoresh* אמר   ⇒   תֲּאֵמֹר   You/she will speak

B. פ-נ

When any prefix letter is added to a פ-נ verb, including the prefix showing the *binyan*, the נ of the root drops and the next letter (i.e. the letter following the dropped נ), almost without fail, takes a *dagesh chazak* to show that the נ has dropped, except when the next letter is a guttural or a ר.

The *shoresh* נטה   ⇒   תִּטֶּה   You will turn

The *shoresh* נפל   ⇒   תִּפְּלִי   You will fall

The *shoresh* נתנ   ⇒   יִתֵּן   He will give

1. In the *pi'el binyan* the פ-נ first root letter does not drop away.

The *shoresh* נשק   ⇒   יְנַשֵּׁק   He will kiss

2. In the *hiph'il binyan* the נ drops away, and there is a י between second and third root letters.

The *shoresh* נפל   ⇒   יַפִּיל   He will fall

3. If a guttural letter follows the dropping נ then the נ does not drop away.

The *shoresh* נחל　　⇒　　תַּנְחִיל　You will bequeath

C. פ-י

1. In the future tense of the *pa'al binyan*, often but not always, the י in the פ position of the *shoresh* will be replaced by the prefix of the future tense with a *tzarah* (under the future tense letter prefix.)

The *shoresh* ידע　　⇒　　תֵּדְעִי　You/she will sit
The *shoresh* ישב　　⇒　　אֵשֵׁב　I will sit

2. In all other binyanim the י in the פ position of the *shoresh* can drop when the *shoresh* has a prefix sign for (1) the *binyan*, (2) the future tense, or (3) the present tense. The י is replaced either by a ו for the active *binyanim* or by a נ for the passive *binyanim*. The ו or the נ in this case can only follow one of six prefix letters; נ, י, ת, א, ה, מ.

The *shoresh* יכח　　⇒　　תּוֹכִיחַ
The *shoresh* יכד　　⇒　　תּוֹכִיד
The *shoresh* ירד　　⇒　　תּוֹרֵד
The *shoresh* יגש　　⇒　　יַגֵּשׁ
　　　　　　　　　or　　יֻגַּשׁ

Note: Generally speaking the ו between the first and second letter of the *shoresh* is a sign of the *pa'al* (פָּעַל) present tense. Occasionally one of the letters; נ, י, ת, א, ה, מ will be a root letter (instead of a prefix), in which case the ו will be a sign of the *pa'al* present tense, and not the sign of a dropping י. More often than not, these six letters will be reserved for the prefix and *binyan* signs, rather than being the first root letter.

The *shoresh* ירד　⇒　יוֹרֵד　(*pa'al* present) He is going down
　　　　　　　⇒　הוֹרִיד　(*hiph'il* past) He brought down
　　　　　　　⇒　מוֹרִיד　(*hiph'il* present) He brings down (also I, You)
　　　　　　　⇒　תּוֹרִיד　(*hiph'il* future) You will bring down
　　　　　　　⇒　יוּרַד　(*hooph'al* future) He will be brought down

D. ע-ו, ע-י

There are many subtle variations of the ע-ו, ע-י dropping letter verbs. Learn these basic rules and you will be well versed.

1. The י and the ו in the ע position of the *shoresh* drop completely in the past and present tense of the *pa'al binyan*. This drop is accompanied by:

   a. A *kametz* under the first letter of the *shoresh* in all parts of the present tense and in the past tense third person, singular and plural.

   > The *shoresh* שומ ⇒ שָׂם He put, I put or You put

   b. A *patach* under the first letter of the *shoresh* in the past tense first and second person singular and plural.

   > The *shoresh* שומ ⇒ שַׂמְתָּ You put
   > The *shoresh* דנת ⇒ דַּנְתִּי I judged

   c. In the future tense of the פָּעַל *binyan* the ו and י of the *shoresh* do not drop, and there is usually a *kamatz* (ָ) under the future tense prefix.

   > The *shoresh* עור ⇒ תָּעִיר You will awaken
   > The *shoresh* קום ⇒ תָּקוּם You arose

2. The י and the ו in the ע position of the *shoresh* drop in the *hiph'il binyan* in all tenses, and are replaced by the י of the *hiph'il binyan* between the first and third letters of the *shoresh*. The *shoresh* will be preceded by the prefix of the *hiph'il binyan*, often with a *tzarah* or *sheva* under the מ prefix in the present tense, or a *patach*, *tzarah* or *chataf-patach* under the ה prefix in the past tense.*

   > The *shoresh* קום ⇒ מֵקִים He establishes
   > The *shoresh* עור ⇒ הֵעִיר He aroused
   > The *shoresh* מות ⇒ הֵמִית He put to death

End of lesson 12

---

* the future tense of ע-ו or ע-י is unique in the future tense of the פָּעַל and הִפְעִיל binyan, finding a ָ (kamatz) under the prefixletter of the future tense. No other form uses a kamatz under the א, ת, י, נ in the future tense.

Lesson 13

Replacing or Dropping
Letters - continued

ל-ה **E.**

1. The ה in the ל position of the *shoresh* changes to a י, in the past tense of the first and second person singular and plural. A *hirik* will be under the letter preceding the replaced ה. The normal past tense ending will then be added after the י, which has replaced the ה.

The *Shoresh*: קנה

Plural	Singular	Person
קָנִינוּ	קָנִיתִי	m, f
קָנִיתֶם	קָנִיתָ	m
קָנִיתֶן	קָנִיתְ	f

Examples

רָאִיתִי

עָשִׂינוּ

2. The ה in the ל position of the *shoresh* does not drop from the third person, masculine singular since there is no suffix in the form. The ה in the third person feminine singular is replaced by a תָ followed by a ה, consistent with the case of a possessive pronoun added to a feminine noun.

Examples

קָנְתָה

הָמְתָה

עָשְׂתָה

3. The ה in the ל position of the *shoresh* is replaced by a ו in the third person masculine and feminine plural, קָנוּ. Similarly, the same laws apply to all future tense verbs that have a suffix in their respective forms. The ה drops and the suffix attaches to the remaining *shoresh* letters. Similarly, the present tense suffix letter ה drops when the present form has a suffix.

Examples

The *shoresh* קנה	$\Rightarrow$	יִקְנוּ	They will buy	
The *shoresh* קנה	$\Rightarrow$	קוֹנִים	They are buying	
The *shoresh* עשה	$\Rightarrow$	עָשׂוּ	They did	

4. In a ל-ה word that demands a direct object or a possessive pronoun ending, the ה changes to a ת, and the word then receives the direct object or possessive noun ending.

5. In the *Chumash* and *Nach*, a ל-ה *shoresh* made into the future tense through the use of a reversing ו, (see below), simply drops the ה.

Examples

וַיֵּרֶד
וַתִּפְתָּ
וָאֵרֶא

6. Later we will learn about the infinitive ל-ה.

Command Form, Reversing Vav (וֹ), The Infinitive & Vital Irregular Verbs

Command Form

The command form is as the name implies a direct instruction for someone or something to initiate an action. You cannot command the first person 'I', nor can you command the third person 'He'. The command form must be directed to the second person 'You' (i.e. the one being spoken to). To form the Hebrew command form, choose the appropriate second person regular verb 'You' masculine or feminine, singular or plural and drop the ת prefix. You will notice that all second person future tense verbs have a ת prefix. Leave the remaining vowels and letters as they are after you remove the ת prefix and its vowel. Notice in the הִתְפַּעֵל, הִפְעִיל and the נִפְעַל *binyan* when the ת drops a ה replaces the dropped ת.

IN EACH *BINYAN* THE COMMAND FORM LOOKS AS FOLLOWS:

נִפְעַל	הִתְפַּעֵל	הִפְעִיל	פִּעֵל	פָּעַל	
תִּשָּׁמֵר⇐הִשָּׁמֵר	תִּתְקַשֵּׁר⇐הִתְקַשֵּׁר	תַּקְצִיר⇐הַקְצֵר	תְּדַבֵּר⇐דַּבֵּר	תִּשְׁמֹר⇐שְׁמֹר	Masc. singular
תִּשָּׁמְרִי⇐הִשָּׁמְרִי	תִּתְקַשְּׁרִי⇐הִתְקַשְּׁרִי	תַּקְצִירִי⇐הַקְצִירִי	תְּדַבְּרִי⇐דַּבְּרִי	תִּשְׁמְרִי⇐שִׁמְרִי	Fem. singular
תִּשָּׁמְרוּ⇐הִשָּׁמְרוּ	תִּתְקַשְּׁרוּ⇐הִתְקַשְּׁרוּ	תַּקְצִירוּ⇐הַקְצִירוּ	תְּדַבְּרוּ⇐דַּבְּרוּ	תִּשְׁמְרוּ⇐שִׁמְרוּ	Masc. plural
	תִּתְקַשֵּׁרְנָה⇐הִתְקַשֵּׁרְנָה	תַּקְצֵירְנָה⇐הַקְצֵרְנָה	תְּדַבֵּרְנָה⇐דַּבֵּרְנָה	תִּשְׁמֹרְנָה⇐שְׁמֹרְנָה	Fem. plural

There is no command form for the *poo'al* and *hooph'al binyanim*.

Reversing Vav (וֹ)

In the *Chumash*, with a few exceptions, when a ו is found as a prefix to a verb in the future tense, or as a prefix to a verb in the past tense, then the verb reverses. The past tense becomes the future tense, while the future tense becomes the past tense.

אָהַבְתָּ = You loved (past tense)	וְאָהַבְתָּ = And you shall love (future tense)
הָיָה = It was (past tense)	וְהָיָה = And it will (shall) be (future tense)
תִּשְׁמֹר = You will guard (future tense)	וְתִּשְׁמֹר = and you guarded (past tense)

* For further details of the reversing ו see appendix III

The Infinitive

The infinitive is the 'to be' form of the verb *shoresh*. It is formed by using the relative *makor* (usually the three letter root, with a unique vowel pattern) of the verb *shoresh* and adding a ל prefix. The infinitive can best be defined as a stop action pictorial of the active verb.

Examples

לִשְׁמֹר = to guard

לֶאֱכֹל = to eat

The vowel pattern of a *binyan* and dropping letters can alter the *shoresh* in the infinitive. The standard vowel patterns are too numerous for this brief presentation. In most cases adding a ל prefix to the **relative *makor*** forms the infinitive. Letters that drop or change in the infinitive are specific cases, and they are not subject to absolute rules. Certain predictable patterns are described below:

7. **פ-י**. The infinitive of some פ-י roots are formed by dropping the י of the root and adding a ת to the remaining root letters and a ל prefix (שֶׁבֶת is the relative makor).

    The *shoresh* ישב ⇒ לָשֶׁבֶת To sit

    The *shoresh* ידע ⇒ לָדַעַת To know

8. **ל-ה**. The infinitive of some ל-ה roots are formed by replacing the ה of the root with a ות and adding the ל prefix.

    The *shoresh* קנה ⇒ לִקְנוֹת To acquire

    The *shoresh* עשה ⇒ לַעֲשׂוֹת To do, to make

9. **פ-נ**. Sometimes the פ-נ can function like a פ-י replacing the נ with a ת at the end of the root and adding the ל prefix.

    The *shoresh* נגש ⇒ לָגֶשֶׁת To approach

    The *shoresh* נתן ⇒ לָתֵת To give

10. In the *niph'al binyan* the נ is replaced by a ה and the ל prefix is added to form the infinitive. Notice the similarity to the future tense with 3 full vowels under the ה and the first 2 root letters.

    The *shoresh* שמר . ⇒ לְהִשָּׁמֵר To be guarded

    The *shoresh* טמן . ⇒ לְהִטָּמֵן To be made concealed

11. In the *hiph'il binyan* the third person, masculine singular, or a very similar form with slight vowel changes, is preceded by the ל prefix to form the infinitive.

The infinitive forms for the *binyanim* are as follows:

Examples

לִשְׁמֹר
לִדְבֹּר
לִשְׁלֹחַ

1. In the *pa'al binyan* the infinitive prefix ל usually has the prefix *hirik* (.) like the future tense prefix letter in combination with the relative *makor* vowelling pattern.

Examples

לְדַבֵּר
לְנַשֵׁק
לְסַפֵּן

2. In the *pi'el binyan* the infinitive prefix ל usually has the prefix *sheva* (ִ) under it as the future and present tense prefix letter joined to the relative *makor*.

Examples

לְהַקְצִיר
לְהַזְכִּיר
לְהַשְׁאִיל

3. In the *hiph'il binyan* the infinitive prefix ל usually has the prefix *sheva* (ְ) under it joined to the relative *makor shoresh* pattern.

Examples

לְהִתְקַשֵּׁר
לְהִתְיַשֵׁב

4. In the *hispa'el binyan* the infinitive prefix ל usually has the prefix *sheva* (ְ) under it with the form of the relative *makor shoresh* pattern from the past tense verb.

Examples

לְהִשָּׁמֵר
לְהִנָּטַל

5. The infinitive form of the *niph'al binyan* has an unusual and distinct pattern. The infinitive prefix ל gets a *sheva* (ְ), while the relative *makor shoresh* has a ה prefix with a *hirik* (.).

6. The *poo'al* and *hooph'al binyanim* do not have infinitive patterns.

Irregular words

Certain words are highly irregular, while being commonly found. The words are unique, not usually following standard patterns due to their common usage they are worth studying on an individual basis. These roots are:

יכל

נתן

היה

צוה

נכה

End of lesson 13

Lesson 14

Rehov Beit Vegan 99, Yerushalayim 02.9920755
1091 River Ave., Lakewood NJ 08701 732.370.3344 fax 1.877.Pirchei (732.367.8168)

Dropping Letter Binyan Quiz

Lesson

14

Person	Number	Gender	Tense	Binyan	Shoresh	Category	Word	Blessing
							יַגִּיד	1
							מֵבִיא	1
							מוֹשִׁיעַ	1
							מַשִׁיב	2
							מוֹרִיד	2
							מַתִּיר	2
							מֵמִית	2
							נַגִּיד	3
							יָמוּשׁ	3
							הֲשִׁיבֵנוּ	5
							הוֹשִׁיעֵנוּ	8
							וְנִוָּשֵׁעָה	8
							נֵבוֹשׁ	13
							תָּשׁוּב	14
							תָּכִין	14
							קִוִּינוּ	15
							מוֹדִים	18
							נוֹדֶה	18
							נָתַתָּ	19

Dropping Letter Binyan Quiz: Answers

Person	Number	Gender	Tense	Binyan	Shoresh	Category	Word	Blessing
3rd	s	m	Future	הפעיל	נגד	פ-נ	יַגִּיד	1
3rd (1/2)	s	m	Present	הפעיל	בוא	ע-ו	מֵבִיא	1
3rd (1/2)	s	m	Present	הפעיל	ישע	פ-י	מוֹשִׁיעַ	1
3rd (1/2)	s	m	Present	הפעיל	נשב	פ-נ	מַשִּׁיב	2
3rd (1/2)	s	m	Present	הפעיל	ירד	פ-י	מוֹרִיד	2
3rd (1/2)	s	m	Present	הפעיל	נתר	פ-נ	מַתִּיר	2
3rd (1/2)	s	m	Present	הפעיל	מות	ע-ו	מֵמִית	2
1st	pl	m,f	Future	הפעיל	נגד	פ-נ	נַגִּיד	3
3rd	s	m	Future	פָּעַל	מוש	ע-ו	יָמוּשׁ	3
			Command	הפעיל	שוב	ע-ו	הֲשִׁיבֵנוּ	5
			Command	הפעיל	ישע	פ-י	הוֹשִׁיעֵנוּ	8
1st	pl	m,f	Future	נפעל	ישע	פ-י	וְנִוָּשֵׁעָה	8
1st	pl	m,f	Future	פָּעַל	בוש	ע-ו	נֵבוֹשׁ	13
2nd	s	m	Future	פָּעַל	שוב	ע-ו	תָּשׁוּב	14
2nd	s	m	Future	הפעיל	כון	ע-ו	תָּכִין	14
1st	pl	m,f	Past	פִּעֵל	קוה	ל-ה	קִוִּינוּ	15
1st	pl	m,f	Present	הפעיל	ידה	פ-י ל-ה	מוֹדִים	18
1st	pl	m,f	Future	הפעיל	ידה	פ-י ל-ה	נוֹדֶה	18
2nd	s	m	Past	פָּעַל	נתן	ל-נ (ל-ה)	נָתַתָּ	19

Lesson 15

Chart 1: Complete Verbs (no dropping letters) in the Seven *Binyanim*

Past Tense									Root קצר					
Plural				Singular										
3rd	2nd (f)	2nd (m)	First	3rd (f)	3rd (m)	2nd (f)	2nd (m)	First	מ	ל	כ	ב	Relative/ Absolute Makor	Category
קָצְרוּ	קְצַרְתֶּן	קְצַרְתֶּם	קָצַרְנוּ	קָצְרָה	קָצַר	קָצַרְתְּ	קָצַרְתָּ	קָצַרְתִּי	מִקְצֹר	לִקְצֹר	כִּקְצֹר	בִּקְצֹר	קָצוֹר, קְצֹר	פָּעַל
קִצְּרוּ	קִצַּרְתֶּן	קִצַּרְתֶּם	קִצַּרְנוּ	קִצְּרָה	קִצֵּר	קִצַּרְתְּ	קִצַּרְתָּ	קִצַּרְתִּי	מִקַּצֵּר	לְקַצֵּר	כְּקַצֵּר	בְּקַצֵּר	קַצֵּר	פִּעֵל
הִקְצִירוּ	הִקְצַרְתֶּן	הִקְצַרְתֶּם	הִקְצַרְנוּ	הִקְצִירָה	הִקְצִיר	הִקְצַרְתְּ	הִקְצַרְתָּ	הִקְצַרְתִּי	מֵהַקְצִר	לְהַקְצִר	כְּהַקְצִר	בְּהַקְצִר	הַקְצֵר, הַקְצִר	הִפְעִיל
הִתְקַצְּרוּ	הִתְקַצַּרְתֶּן	הִתְקַצַּרְתֶּם	הִתְקַצַּרְנוּ	הִתְקַצְּרָה	הִתְקַצֵּר	הִתְקַצַּרְתְּ	הִתְקַצַּרְתָּ	הִתְקַצַּרְתִּי	הִתְקַצֵּר	לְהִתְקַצֵּר	כְּהִתְקַצֵּר	בְּהִתְקַצֵּר	הִתְקַצֵּר	הִתְפַּעֵל
נִקְצְרוּ	נִקְצַרְתֶּן	נִקְצַרְתֶּם	נִקְצַרְנוּ	נִקְצְרָה	נִקְצַר	נִקְצַרְתְּ	נִקְצַרְתָּ	נִקְצַרְתִּי	מֵהִקָּצֵר	לְהִקָּצֵר	כְּהִקָּצֵר	בְּהִקָּצֵר	נִקְצוֹר, הִקָּצֵר	נִפְעַל
קֻצְּרוּ	קֻצַּרְתֶּן	קֻצַּרְתֶּם	קֻצַּרְנוּ	קֻצְּרָה	קֻצַּר	קֻצַּרְתְּ	קֻצַּרְתָּ	קֻצַּרְתִּי	None	None	None	None	קֻצּוֹר	פֻּעַל
הֻקְצְרוּ	הֻקְצַרְתֶּן	הֻקְצַרְתֶּם	הֻקְצַרְנוּ	הֻקְצְרָה	הֻקְצַר	הֻקְצַרְתְּ	הֻקְצַרְתָּ	הֻקְצַרְתִּי	None	None	None	None	הֻקְצַר	הֻפְעַל

	Command (imperative)				Future Tense										Present Tense			
	Plural		Singular		Plural					Singular					Plural		Singular	
	F	M	F	M	3rd (f)	3rd (m)	2nd (f)	2nd (m)	First	3rd (f)	3rd (m)	2nd (f)	2nd (m)	First	F	M	F	M
פָּעַל	קְצֹרְנָה	קִצְרוּ	קִצְרִי	קְצֹר	תִּקְצֹרְנָה	יִקְצְרוּ	תִּקְצֹרְנָה	תִּקְצְרוּ	נִקְצֹר	תִּקְצֹר	יִקְצֹר	תִּקְצְרִי	תִּקְצֹר	אֶקְצֹר	קוֹצְרוֹת	קוֹצְרִים	קוֹצֶרֶת (קוֹצְרָה)	קוֹצֵר
פִּעֵל	קַצֵּרְנָה	קַצְּרוּ	קַצְּרִי	קַצֵּר	תְּקַצֵּרְנָה	יְקַצְּרוּ	תְּקַצֵּרְנָה	תְּקַצְּרוּ	נְקַצֵּר	תְּקַצֵּר	יְקַצֵּר	תְּקַצְּרִי	תְּקַצֵּר	אֲקַצֵּר	מְקַצְּרוֹת	מְקַצְּרִים	מְקַצֶּרֶת	מְקַצֵּר
הִפְעִיל	הַקְצֵרְנָה	הַקְצִרוּ	הַקְצִרִי	הַקְצֵר	תַּקְצֵרְנָה	יַקְצִירוּ	תַּקְצֵרְנָה	תַּקְצִירוּ	נַקְצִיר	תַּקְצִיר	יַקְצִיר	תַּקְצִירִי	תַּקְצִיר	אַקְצִיר	מַקְצִירוֹת	מַקְצִירִים	מַקְצֶרֶת (מַקְצִירָה)	מַקְצִיר
הִתְפַּעֵל	הִתְקַצֵּרְנָה	הִתְקַצְּרוּ	הִתְקַצְּרִי	הִתְקַצֵּר	תִּתְקַצֵּרְנָה	יִתְקַצְּרוּ	תִּתְקַצֵּרְנָה	תִּתְקַצְּרוּ	נִתְקַצֵּר	תִּתְקַצֵּר	יִתְקַצֵּר	תִּתְקַצְּרִי	תִּתְקַצֵּר	אֶתְקַצֵּר	מִתְקַצְּרוֹת	מִתְקַצְּרִים	מִתְקַצֶּרֶת (מִתְקַצְּרָה)	מִתְקַצֵּר
נִפְעַל	הִקָּצַרְנָה	הִקָּצְרוּ	הִקָּצְרִי	הִקָּצֵר	תִּקָּצַרְנָה	יִקָּצְרוּ	תִּקָּצַרְנָה	תִּקָּצְרוּ	נִקָּצֵר	תִּקָּצֵר	יִקָּצֵר	תִּקָּצְרִי	תִּקָּצֵר	אֶקָּצֵר	נִקְצָרוֹת	נִקְצָרִים	נִקְצֶרֶת (נִקְצָרָה)	נִקְצָר
פֻּעַל	None	None	None	None	תְּקֻצַּרְנָה	יְקֻצְּרוּ	תְּקֻצַּרְנָה	תְּקֻצְּרוּ	נְקֻצַּר	תְּקֻצַּר	יְקֻצַּר	תְּקֻצְּרִי	תְּקֻצַּר	אֲקֻצַּר	מְקֻצָּרוֹת	מְקֻצָּרִים	מְקֻצֶּרֶת	מְקֻצָּר
הֻפְעַל	None	None	None	None	תֻּקְצַרְנָה	יֻקְצְרוּ	תֻּקְצַרְנָה	תֻּקְצְרוּ	נֻקְצַר	תֻּקְצַר	יֻקְצַר	תֻּקְצְרִי	תֻּקְצַר	אֻקְצַר	מֻקְצָרוֹת	מֻקְצָרִים	מֻקְצֶרֶת	מֻקְצָר

Chart 2: Irregular Verbs (with dropping letters) in the *Pa'al*, *Pi'el* and *Hiph'il Binyanim*

Past Tense									Root							
Plural				Singular												
3rd	2nd (f)	2nd (m)	First	3rd (f)	3rd (m)	2nd (f)	2nd (m)	First	מ	ל	כ	ב	Relative/ Absolute Makor	Root	Category	
אָכְלוּ	אֲכַלְתֶּן	אֲכַלְתֶּם	אָכַלְנוּ	אָכְלָה	אָכַל	אָכַלְתְּ	אָכַלְתָּ	אָכַלְתִּי	מֵאֲכֹל	לֶאֱכֹל	כֶּאֱכֹל	בַּאֲכֹל	אָכוֹל, אֱכֹל	אכל	פָּעַל פ"א	פָּעַל
יָשְׁבוּ	יְשַׁבְתֶּן	יְשַׁבְתֶּם	יָשַׁבְנוּ	יָשְׁבָה	יָשַׁב	יָשַׁבְתְּ	יָשַׁבְתָּ	יָשַׁבְתִּי	מִשֶּׁבֶת	לָשֶׁבֶת	כְּשֶׁבֶת	בְּשֶׁבֶת	יָשׁוֹב, שֶׁבֶת	ישב	פָּעַל פ"י	
נָפְלוּ	נְפַלְתֶּן	נְפַלְתֶּם	נָפַלְנוּ	נָפְלָה	נָפַל	נָפַלְתְּ	נָפַלְתָּ	נָפַלְתִּי	מִנְּפֹל	לִנְפֹּל	כִּנְפֹל	בִּנְפֹל	נָפוֹל, נְפֹל	נפל	פָּעַל פ"נ	
קָמוּ	קַמְתֶּן	קַמְתֶּם	קַמְנוּ	קָמָה	קָם	קַמְתְּ	קַמְתָּ	קַמְתִּי	מִקּוּם	לָקוּם	כְּקוּם	בְּקוּם	קוֹם, קוּם	קומ	פָּעַל ע"ו	
רָאוּ	רְאִיתֶן	רְאִיתֶם	רָאִינוּ	רָאֲתָה	רָאָה	רָאִית	רָאִיתָ	רָאִיתִי	מֵרְאוֹת	לִרְאוֹת	כִּרְאוֹת	בִּרְאוֹת	רָאֹה, רְאוֹת	רסה	פָּעַל ל"ה	
קָרְאוּ	קְרָאתֶן	קְרָאתֶם	קָרָאנוּ	קָרְאָה	קָרָא	קָרָאת	קָרָאתָ	קָרָאתִי	מִקְּרֹא	לִקְרֹא	כִּקְרֹא	בִּקְרֹא	קָרוֹא, קְרֹא	קרא	פָּעַל ל"א	
צִוּוּ	צִוִּיתֶן	צִוִּיתֶם	צִוִּינוּ	צִוְּתָה	צִוָּה	צִוִּית	צִוִּיתָ	צִוִּיתִי	מִצַּוּוֹת	לְצַוּוֹת	כְּצַוּוֹת	בְּצַוּוֹת	צַוּוֹת	צוה	פִּעֵל ל"ה,ע"ו	פִּעֵל
הֶאֱכִילוּ	הֶאֱכַלְתֶּן	הֶאֱכַלְתֶּם	הֶאֱכַלְנוּ	הֶאֱכִילָה	הֶאֱכִיל	הֶאֱכַלְתְּ	הֶאֱכַלְתָּ	הֶאֱכַלְתִּי	מֵהַאֲכִיל	לְהַאֲכִיל	כְּהַאֲכִיל	בְּהַאֲכִיל	הַאֲכִיל, הַאֲכֵל	אכל	הִפְעִיל פ"א	הִפְעִיל
הוֹרִידוּ	הוֹרַדְתֶּן	הוֹרַדְתֶּם	הוֹרַדְנוּ	הוֹרִידָה	הוֹרִיד	הוֹרַדְתְּ	הוֹרַדְתָּ	הוֹרַדְתִּי	מֵהוֹרִיד	לְהוֹרִיד	כְּהוֹרִיד	בְּהוֹרִיד	הוֹרֵד, הוֹרִיד	ירד	הִפְעִיל פ"י	
הִפִּילוּ	הִפַּלְתֶּן	הִפַּלְתֶּם	הִפַּלְנוּ	הִפִּילָה	הִפִּיל	הִפַּלְתְּ	הִפַּלְתָּ	הִפַּלְתִּי	מֵהַפִּיל	לְהַפִּיל	כְּהַפִּיל	בְּהַפִּיל	הַפֵּל, הַפִּיל	נפל	הִפְעִיל פ"נ	
הֵקִימוּ	הֲקִימוֹתֶן	הֲקִימוֹתֶם	הֲקִימוֹנוּ	הֵקִימָה	הֵקִים	הֲקִימוֹת	הֲקִימוֹתָ	הֲקִימוֹתִי	מֵהָקִים	לְהָקִים	כְּהָקִים	בְּהָקִים	הָקֵם, הָקִים	קומ	הִפְעִיל ע"ו-י"	
הֶרְאוּ	הֶרְאֵיתֶן	הֶרְאֵיתֶם	הֶרְאִינוּ	הֶרְאֲרָה	הֶרְאִית	הֶרְאֵית	הֶרְאֵיתָ	הֶרְאֵיתִי	מֵהַרְאוֹת	לְהַרְאוֹת	כְּהַרְאוֹת	בְּהַרְאוֹת	הַרְאֵה, הַרְאוֹת	ראה	הִפְעִיל ל"ה	

		Command (imperative)				Future Tense										Present Tense			
		Plural		Singular		Plural					Singular					Plural		Singular	
		F	M	F	M	3rd (f)	3rd (m)	2nd (f)	2nd (m)	First	3rd (f)	3rd (m)	2nd (f)	2nd (m)	First	F	M	F	M
פָּעַל	פָּעַל פ"א	אֱכֹלְנָה	אִכְלוּ	אִכְלִי	אֱכֹל	תֹּאכַלְנָה	יֹאכְלוּ	תֹּאכַלְנָה	תֹּאכְלוּ	נֹאכַל	תֹּאכַל	יֹאכַל	תֹּאכְלִי	תֹּאכַל	אֹכַל	אוֹכְלוֹת	אוֹכְלִים	אוֹכֶלֶת (אוֹכְלָה)	אוֹכֵל
	פָּעַל פ"י	שֵׁבְנָה	שְׁבוּ	שְׁבִי	שֵׁב	תֵּשַׁבְנָה	יֵשְׁבוּ	תֵּשַׁבְנָה	תֵּשְׁבוּ	נֵשֵׁב	תֵּשֵׁב	יֵשֵׁב	תֵּשְׁבִי	תֵּשֵׁב	אֵשֵׁב	יוֹשְׁבוֹת	יוֹשְׁבִים	יוֹשֶׁבֶת (יוֹשְׁבָה)	יוֹשֵׁב
	פָּעַל פ"נ	נְפֹלְנָה	נִפְלוּ	נִפְלִי	נְפֹל	תִּפֹּלְנָה	יִפְּלוּ	תִּפֹּלְנָה	תִּפְּלוּ	נִפֹּל	תִּפֹּל	יִפֹּל	תִּפְּלִי	תִּפֹּל	אֶפֹּל	נוֹפְלוֹת	נוֹפְלִים	נוֹפֶלֶת (נוֹפְלָה)	נוֹפֵל
	פָּעַל פ"ו	תְּקֻמְנָה	קוּמוּ	קוּמִי	קוּם	תָּקֹמְנָה	יָקוּמוּ	תָּקֹמְנָה	תָּקוּמוּ	נָקוּם	תָּקוּם	יָקוּם	תָּקוּמִי	תָּקוּם	אָקוּם	קָמוֹת	קָמִים	קָמָה	קָם
	פָּעַל ל"ה	רְאֶנָה	רְאוּ	רְאִי	רְאֵה	תִּרְאֶינָה	יִרְאוּ	תִּרְאֶינָה	תִּרְאוּ	נִרְאֶה	תִּרְאֶה	יִרְאֶה	תִּרְאִי	תִּרְאֶה	אֶרְאֶה	רוֹאוֹת	רוֹאִים	רֹאָה	רוֹאֶה
	פָּעַל ל"א	קְרֶאנָה	קִרְאוּ	קִרְאִי	קְרָא	תִּקְרֶאנָה	יִקְרְאוּ	תִּקְרֶאנָה	תִּקְרְאוּ	נִקְרָא	תִּקְרָא	יִקְרָא	תִּקְרְאִי	תִּקְרָא	אֶקְרָא	קוֹרְאוֹת	קוֹרְאִים	קוֹרֵאת (קוֹרְאָה)	קוֹרֵא
פִּעֵל	פִּעֵל ל"ה	תְּצַוֶּינָה	צַוּוּ	צַוִּי	צַוֵּה	תְּצַוֶּינָה	יְצַוּוּ	תְּצַוֶּינָה	תְּצַוּוּ	נְצַוֶּה	תְּצַוֶּה	יְצַוֶּה	תְּצַוִּי	תְּצַוֶּה	אֲצַוֶּה	מְצַוּוֹת	מְצַוִּים	מְצַוָּה	מְצַוֶּה
הִפְעִיל	הִפְעִיל פ"א	תַּאֲכֵלְנָה	הַאֲכִילוּ	הַאֲכִילִי	הַאֲכֵל	תַּאֲכֵלְנָה	יַאֲכִילוּ	תַּאֲכֵלְנָה	תַּאֲכִילוּ	נַאֲכִיל	תַּאֲכִיל	יַאֲכִיל	תַּאֲכִילִי	תַּאֲכִיל	אַאֲכִיל	מַאֲכִילוֹת	מַאֲכִילִים	מַאֲכֶלֶת (מַאֲכִילָה)	מַאֲכִיל
	הִפְעִיל פ"י	תּוֹרֵדְנָה	הוֹרִידוּ	הוֹרִידִי	הוֹרֵד	תּוֹרֵדְנָה	יוֹרִידוּ	תּוֹרֵדְנָה	תּוֹרִידוּ	נוֹרִיד	תּוֹרִיד	יוֹרִיד	תּוֹרִידִי	תּוֹרִיד	אוֹרִיד	מוֹרִידוֹת	מוֹרִידִים	מוֹרֶדֶת (מוֹרִידָה)	מוֹרִיד
	הִפְעִיל פ"ן	תַּפֵּלְנָה	הַפִּילוּ	הַפִּילִי	הַפֵּל	תַּפֵּלְנָה	יַפִּילוּ	תַּפֵּלְנָה	תַּפִּילוּ	נַפִּיל	תַּפִּיל	יַפִּיל	תַּפִּילִי	תַּפִּיל	אַפִּיל	מַפִּילוֹת	מַפִּילִים	מַפֶּלֶת (מַפִּילָה)	מַפִּיל
	הִפְעִיל ע"ו	הָקֵמְנָה	הָקִימוּ	הָקִימִי	הָקֵם	תְּקֵמְנָה	יָקִימוּ	תְּקֵמְנָה	תָּקִימוּ	נָקִים	תָּקִים	יָקִים	תָּקִימִי	תָּקִים	אָקִים	מְקִימוֹת	מְקִימִים	מְקִימָה	מֵקִים
	הִפְעִיל ל"ה	הַרְאֶינָה	הַרְאוּ	הַרְאִי	הַרְאֵה	תַּרְאֶנָה	יַרְאוּ	תַּרְאֶנָה	תַּרְאוּ	נַרְאֶה	תַּרְאֶה	יַרְאֶה	תַּרְאִי	תַּרְאֶה	אַרְאֶה	מַרְאוֹת	מַרְאִים	מַרְאָה	מַרְאֶה

Prefix Chart

Prefix	Past	Present	Future	Noun/Adj	Poss. end Direct Object	Special Notes
א			I will			
אֶ			*Hispa'el* I will			
ה				In, with, at on, among, within, into, by, of as when		
ה	*hiph'il hooph'al*	Definite noun		The definitive or interrogative		
התּ	*hispa'el*					
ו	Reversing ו (and)	And	Reversing ו (and)	And	ו Changes past to future, and future to past in דבר	
י			He will			
יXXXו			They will (*m,pf*)			
יתּ			*Hispa'el* He will			
יXXXו			*Hispa'el* They will			
כּ				Like, as. Similarly		
כשׁ				כְּ + noun/adj = when		
ל				To, for		w/verb *makor* forms infinitive
מ		*pi'el, hiph'il, hispa'el, poo'al, hooph'al*		From, of more than, since		Sign of a noun
מתּ		*hispa'el*				
נ	*niph'al*	*niph'al*	We will			Sign of a noun
נתּ			*hispa'el* we will			
שׁ				That, which, who, whom, because, since for		
תּ			You (*m,s*) She (*f,s*)			
תXXXי			You will (*f,s*)			
תתּ			You will (*m,s*) She will (*f,s*)			
תXXXX			You will (*f,pf*)			
תXXXXנה			You/they will (*f,pf*)			
תXXXX *hispa'el*			You will (*m,pf*)			
תXXXXנה *hispa'el*			You/they will (*f,pf*)			

Note: A shaded box means noun/adjective/pronoun prefix

Infix Chart

Infix	Past	Present	Future	Noun/Adj	Poss. end Direct Object	Special Notes
xxׂîx		(m & f, s & pl)		Noun, adj.		
xîxx				Adjective		
xîxx				Noun, adj.		
xׂîxxה	Hiph'il (3 pers)	Hiph'il w/present tense forms	Hiph'il w/future tense prefix	Infinitive, absolute, noun/adj.		
xׂxx				Noun, adj.		
הxׂîxx				Gerund		Gerund is noun form of verb ending in 'ing'
הxîxx						

Suffix Chart

Suffix	Past	Present	Future	Noun/Adj	Poss. end Direct Object	Special Notes
הָ	She was	She is		Replaces ה prefix noun/adj. (f,s)	Hers, her	Her = obj. of prep.
ו	They (m & f, pl)		They, you (m,pl), command form		His (ו), him (ו)	Her = obj. of prep.
הֹ		(f,pl)		(f,pl)	His or him	
הֹן/					Their, them (f,pl)	
×ָ					Me, my mine (m & f, s)	
×ֶ					Me, my mine (m)	
×ֶ				Construct noun (m,pl)		
×ָֹ	First person (m & f, s)					
י			Command form (f,s)			
×ׂxxי (final ×כ) ך		(m,pl)	(m,pl)		You (m & f, s)	Obj or prep
כֹ					You (m,pl)	Obj or prep
כֶ					You (f,pl)	Obj or prep
ם					You, them theirs (m,pl)	Obj or prep
הֹם					You, them theirs (m,pl)	Obj or prep
הֹ			You/they will (f,pl)		Her = direct object	
תֹ You (m & f, s)						
הֹם You (m,pl)						
נו We (m & f, pl)					We, our, ours (m & f, pl)	
הֹן You (f,pl)						
×ת				Construct noun (f,s)		
×ת	(f,s)			(f,s)		

Aramaic Grammar for Gemorah and Onkelos

Verb Forms

Passive	Causative	Intensive	Simple	See notes on bottom of page	
איתפעל	אפעל	פעל	פעל	Past עבר	
נתפעל	נפעל	נפעל	ניפע(ו)ל	Future עתיד	
מי(ת)פעל	מפעל	מפעל	פע(י)ל	Present הווה	
לאי(ת)פעולי	לאפעולי	(ל)פעולי	(ל)מיפעולי	Infinitive שם פועל	

Noun Forms

Feminine		Masculine		See notes on bottom of page	
Plural	Singular	Plural	Singular		
אן	אה/אא	אין/אי		A book	General נפרד
את	את	אי	XXX	The book of Shmos	Construct נסמך
אתא	אתא אתי/אא	יא	אא	The book	Specific ידוע

Verb Tenses, Gender and Person

Present		Future		Past		See notes on bottom of page	
Plural	Singular	Plural	Singular	Plural	Singular		
		נX	אX	נא/ן	אית/אי/את	Masculine	First Person
		נX	אX	נא/ן	אית/אי/את	Feminine	
		תאון/תאתון/תא	תא	אתון/אתו	את	Masculine	Second Person
		תאן/תאתון/תאן	תאין/אי	אתון/(אתן)	את	Feminine	
אין		נאו/לאו/לאי/ליאון	יא/לא/נא	או/XXאו	Masculine	Third Person
אן	אה/אא	ת/לאן	תא	אן/אא	אתא/אא/אה	Feminine	

Pronouns

I	אנא
You	את/אנת
He	ניהו/איהו
She	ניהי/איהי
We	אנחנא/אנן
You (pl)	אתו/אתון
They (m)	אינהו/נינהו/אינהו/אינון
They (f)	אינהי/נינהי

Demonstratives

This (m)	האי/דין
This (f)	הא/דא
These	הני/אילן
That (m)	האיך/ההוא
That (f)	הך/ההיא
Those	הנהו/הנך/הני
This/That	אידי/ואידי
This (comp.)	אידך
That (comp.)	אינך

Possessive Pronouns
(Also Direct Objects & Objects of Preposition)

My	דידי
Your	דידך
His	דידיה
Her	דידה
Our	דידנא/דידן
Your (pl)	דידכון/דידכו
Their (m)	דידהון/דידהו
Their (f)	דידהי

Numbers

1	חדא/חד
2	תרתי/תרי/תרין
3	תלת/תלתא
6	שית/שתא
8	תמני/תמניא
10	עסר/עסרא
½	פלגא
⅓	תתא
¼	רבעה
⅙	שחית

Aramaic .... Hebrew

Aramaic	Hebrew
ת	שׁ
ר	נ
ד	ז
ע	צ
ט	צ

Notes for above charts:

X = The 3 letter root of a word.

Bold letters indicate the identifying signs for tense and level of activity.

( ) = Letters which are found less frequently as identifying signs for tense and level of activity

Appendix I

Rehov Beit Vegan 99, Yerushalayim 02.644.6376
1091 River Ave., Lakewood NJ 08701 732.370.3344 fax 1.877.Pirchei (732.367.8168)

Appendix I

This list of 220 verb roots are the most popular verb roots as found in the Hebrew Bible. The roots are divided into four groupings and each group is in alphabetical order.

1. Words which occur between 500 – 5000 times in the chumash. (#1 - #26)
2. words that occur 200 – 500 times in the chumash. (#27 - #63)
3. words that occur 100 – 200 times. (#64 - #123)
4. words that occur 50 to 100 times. (#124 - #220)

Notice: The words in each category are in alphabetical order, not necessary in order of frequency.

500 – 5000 times

1. אכל .... food/eat
2. אמר .... speak/say
3. בוא .... go, come
4. דבר .... speak, word
5. היה .... to be, happen
6. הלך .... walk, go
7. ידע .... know
8. ילד .... birth, child
9. יצא .... go out, exit
10. ישב .... dwell, sit
11. לקח .... take
12. מות .... die, death
13. נשא .... lift, carry
14. נתן .... give, put
15. עבר .... pass, transgress
16. עלה .... go up, elevate
17. עמד .... stand
18. עשה .... do, make
19. צוה .... command
20. קום .... stand, establish
21. קרא .... read, call
22. ראה .... see, look
23. שים .... place, put
24. שוב .... return
25. שלח .... send
26. שמע .... hear, listen

200 – 500 times

27. אהב .... love
28. אסף .... gather
29. בנה .... build
30. בקש .... seek, inquire
31. ברך .... bless
32. זכר .... remember, mention
33. חזק .... strong, grasp
34. חטא .... offend, sin
35. חיה .... live
36. יכל .... be able
37. יסף .... add
38. ירא .... fear
39. ירד .... descend
40. ירש .... inherit
41. ישע .... victorious, save
42. כון .... prepare, firm
43. כלה .... finish
44. כרת .... cut
45. כתב .... write
46. מלא .... fill, full
47. מלך .... rule, king
48. מצא .... find
49. נגד .... tell, oppose
50. נטה .... reach out, extend
51. נכה .... strike, hit
52. נפל .... fall
53. נצל .... rescue
54. סור .... turn aside
55. עבד .... slave, work, serve
56. ענה .... answer
57. פקד .... count, command
58. רבה .... increase, numerous

59. רום.............high, exalted
60. שכב.............lie down
61. שמר.............guard
62. שפט.............judge
63. שתה.............feast, drink

```
┌─────────────────┐
│  100 – 200 times │
└─────────────────┘
```

64. אבד.............destroy, lose
65. אמן.............trust, stable
66. בוש.............shame, embarrass
67. בטח.............trust
68. בין.............understand
69. בכה.............cry
70. גאל.............redeem
71. גדל.............grow, great
72. גור.............dwell (as a foreigner)
73. גלה.............go away, uncover
74. דרש.............seek
75. הלל.............praise
76. הרג.............kill
77. זבח.............slaughter
78. חלל.............defile
79. חנה.............camp
80. חשב.............think, consider
81. טמא.............impure
82. ידה.............thanks, throw, shoot, praise
83. יטב.............good
84. יתר.............left over
85. כבד.............heavy, honor
86. כסה.............cover, conceal

87. כפר.............atone, appease, lid
88. לבש.............dress, wear
89. לחם.............fight, battle
90. לכד.............catch, capture
91. נבא.............prophecy
92. נגע.............touch, hurt
93. נגש.............approach
94. נוס.............flee
95. נסע.............travel, break camp
96. סבב.............encircle, around
97. ספר.............count, book, tell
98. עזב.............forsake
99. פנה.............turn, face
100. פתח.............open, door
101. קבץ.............gather, collect
102. קבר.............bury, grave
103. קדש.............holy, sanctify
104. קטר.............smoke, burn sac
105. קרב.............near
106. רדף.............pursue
107. רוץ.............run
108. רעה.............graze, shepherd
109. שׂמח.............joy
110. שׂנא.............hate, jealous
111. שׂרף.............burn
112. שאל.............ask
113. שאר.............remain
114. שבע.............swear, sevens
115. שבר.............break
116. שחה.............bow down

117. שחת .... destroy, ruin
118. שכח .... forget
119. שכן .... dwell, settle
120. שלך .... throw down, away
121. שלם .... whole, complete, peace, joy
122. שפך .... pour, spill
123. שרת .... minister, serve

50 – 100 times

124. אבה .... want, willing
125. אחז .... seize, hold
126. אסר .... bind, prison
127. ארר .... curse
128. בחר .... choose
129. בלע .... swallow
130. בער .... burn
131. בקע .... split
132. ברא .... create
133. ברח .... flee
134. דבק .... cling, stick
135. דרך .... tread, way
136. הפך .... overturn
137. זנה .... illicit
138. זעק .... cry out
139. זרע .... sow, seed
140. חדל .... end, cease
141. חול .... dance, whirl
142. חזה .... see, perceive
143. חלה .... weak, sick
144. חלק .... divide, portion

145. חנן .... gracious
146. חפץ .... want, pleasure
147. חרה .... hot, angry
148. חרם .... ban, destruction
149. חרש .... plow, silent
150. חתת .... terrified
151. טהר .... pure
152. יבש .... dry
153. יכח .... rebuke
154. יעץ .... advise, counsel
155. יצק .... pour out, spread
156. יצר .... form, create
157. ירה .... law, teach
158. כבס .... wash
159. כעס .... anger, incite
160. כשל .... stumble
161. לין .... spend the night
162. למד .... learn, teach
163. מאס .... reject
164. מדד .... measure
165. מהר .... hurry
166. מכר .... sell
167. מלט .... escape
168. משח .... anointed
169. משל .... govern, rule
170. נבט .... gaze
171. נדח .... scatter, banish
172. נוח .... rest, settle
173. נחל .... inherit
174. נטע .... plant

4

175. נכר .... recognize, alien

176. נצב .... stand, setup

177. נצח .... supervise, glory

178. נצר .... keep watch, comply

179. נשׂג .... catch up

180. סגר .... deliver, close

181. סתר .... hide, conceal

182. עוּר .... awake, getup

183. עזר .... help

184. ערך .... arrange, order

185. פדה .... redeem

186. פוּץ .... scatter

187. פלא .... difficult, wonder

188. פלל .... pray

189. פעל .... do, make

190. פרד .... separate

191. פרשׂ .... spread out

192. צלח .... succeed, strong

193. צפה .... watch, look out

194. צרר .... distress, conflict

195. קלל .... small, curse

196. קנה .... acquire

197. קרע .... tear

198. רחם .... mercy, compassion

199. רחץ .... wash, rinse

200. רחק .... far away

201. ריב .... quarrel, lawsuit

202. רכב .... ride, chariot

203. רנן .... shout with joy, moan, whimper

204. רעע .... bad, evil, harm

205. רפא .... heal

206. רצה .... pleased, like

207. שׂבע .... satisfied

208. שׂכל .... understands

209. שבת .... cease, stop

210. שדד .... violent, devastate

211. שחט .... kill

212. שיר .... sing

213. שית .... put, set

214. שכם .... rise early

215. שמד .... exterminate

216. שׁמם .... deserted, desolate

217. שקה .... give drink, water

218. תמם .... complete, blameless

219. תפש .... capture

220. תקע .... blow, drive

Appendix II

Rehov Beit Vegan 99, Yerushalayim 02.644.6376
1091 River Ave., Lakewood NJ 08701 732.370.3344 fax 1.877.Pirchei (732.367.8168)

Appendix II

Rules of the *kamatz katan* (short *kamatz*)

According to the rules of syllables it is possible to differentiate between a short *kamatz* and long *kamatz*. These are the guidelines for *kamatz katan*:

a. If the *kamatz* appears in a closed unaccented syllable.

 Examples: אָרְ-כּוֹ ,הָשְׁ-לַךְ ,בְּשָׁמְ-רִי ,אָזְ-נַיִם

b. If the *kamatz katan* is derived from a deficient *holam*.

 Examples: צֹרֶךְ ◀— צָרְכִּי

 חֹדֶשׁ ◀— חָדְשְׁכֶם

c. If the *kamatz katan* preceed and furtive *kamatz* (*chataf kamatz*)

 Examples: מָחֳרַת , צָהֳרַיִם, אָהֳלִי

d. If the *kamatz katan* replace furtive *kamatz* under a guttural.

 Example: הָעֳמְדוּ

1

Appendix III

Rehov Beit Vegan 99, Yerushalayim 02.644.6376
1091 River Ave., Lakewood NJ 08701 732.370.3344 fax 1.877.Pirchei (732.367.8168)

Appendix III

The Vav Conversive (הַהִפּוּךְ)

The conversive vav precides a past tense verb for which becomes translated in the future, or a future tense verb form that translates in the past.

    a.   The vowel of the conversive ו converting past into future is the same as the plain conjunctive vowel pattern:

             Examples: וַעֲשִׂיתֶם, וּשְׁמַרְתֶּם, וְאָמַר

    b.   The conversant vav converting a future form into the past is a *patach* and the letter after the ו gets a *dagesh chazak*:

             Examples: וַתְּדַבֵּר, וַיֹּאמֶר

    c.   Before an א the conversive ו has a *kamatz*:

             Examples: וָאֹמַר, וָאֵלֵךְ

Appendix IV

Rehov Beit Vegan 99, Yerushalayim 02.644.6376
1091 River Ave., Lakewood NJ 08701 732.370.3344 fax 1.877.Pirchei (732.367.8168)

Appendix IV

Here is a wonderful exercise to help you practice your reading acclerity. The 5 letters of the name אליהו combined with the vowels of the name. Run thru all the possible combinations of letters & vowels. Pronounce this difficult and stimulating reading exercise.*

אֵיוֹהָל	אֵיוֹלָה	אֵיָהֹלוּ	אֵיָהוֹל	אֵיָהֹיִ	אֶלוֹהִי	אֵלִיָהוּ	אֵלְהָיו	אֵלֹהוִּ	אֵלִיָוה	אֵלִיָהוּ
אֹולְהִיָ	אוּלְיָה	אֹהלִיו	אֶהלֹוִּ	אֶהָיֹול	אֶהָלוּ	אֶהֹולְי	אֶהוִיָל	אֶהוֹיל	אֵילָוה	אֵילָהוּ
לִיָאֹוה	לִיָאֵהֹו	לִיֹהָא	לִיֹהָא	לִיָהָאו	לְיֹהָוא	לִיֹהָלְי	אֹוהֵלֹי	אֹוהֵלֹי	אֹויֹלָה	אֹויָהֶל
לֹויָאֶה	לֹויָהֵא	לֹואֵהִי	לֹואֵיָה	לֹואֵיָהו	לְהֹיָוא	לְהֹיָוא	לְהָאֹיו	לְהָאֹיִו	לְהֹויָא	לְהֹואֵי
יָהֹולָא	יָהֹואֵל	לֵאֹהֹיו	לֵאֵהֹיו	לֵאֹהִי	לֵאֹויָה	לֵאֹיָוה	לֵאָיָהוּ	לֵאֹיָיָא	לֹוהָיָא	לֹוהָאֵי
יֹוהָלָא	יֹוהָאֵל	יֹולֵאָה	יֹולֵהָא	יֹואֵהָל	יֹואֵלְה	יֹואֵלָוו	יָהֹלוֹא	יָהֹלֹוא	יָהֵאֹול	יָהֵאֹלוּ
יֹלֹוהָא	יָלֹואֵה	יָלֹהָאו	יָלֹהָוא	יָאֹוהֵל	יָאֹולָה	יָאֵהֹלוּ	יָאֵהֹול	יָאֵלוֹה	יָאֵלָהוּ	
הָאֵלֹיִ	הָאֵלִיו	הֹויָלֵא	הֹויָאֵל	הֹולֵאֵי	הֹולֵיָא	הֹואֵיָל	הֹואֵלֹי	יֹלָאוֹה	יָלָאֶהוּ	
הֹלֹויָא	הֹלֹואֵי	הֵלִיָאו	הָלְיֹוא	הָלָאֹוִי	הָלְאֵיו	הָלֹויָל	הָאֹולְי	הָאֹוִילֹ	הָאֹיוֹל	
וֹאֵיָלָה	וֹאֵיָהִי	וֹאֵלְהִי	וֹאֵלִיָה	וֹאֵלְהָאו	וֹלִיָהָא	וֹלֵאֵהִי	וֹלָאֵיָה	הָיֹולֵא	הָיֹואֵל	
וֹיָאֹהָל	וֹיָאֵלָה	וֹלְהִיָא	וֹלְהֹיָא	וֹלְהֹאִי	וֹלְיָאֵה	וֹלִיָהָא	וֹלָאֵהִי	וָאֵהִיל	וָאֵהֹלי	
וֹהֵיָלָא	וֹהֵיָאֵל	וֹהֵלִיָא	וֹהֵלֹאֵי	וֹהָאֵיל	וֹהָאֵלִי	וִיהָאֵל	וִיהָאֵל	וִילָאֵה	וִילָהָא	
אֵלִיָהוּ	אֵלִיָהוּ	אֵלִיָהוּ	אֵלִיָהוּ	אֵלִיָהוּ	אֵלִיָהוּ	אֵלִיָהוּ	אֵלִיָהוּ	אֵלִיָהוּ	אֵלִיָהוּ	

* If you feel down or depressed try reading these 130 words as fast as possible and I will also guarantee you a smile on your lips by the second line and a good laugh by line 3...

SELF EVALUATION SHEETS

Rehov Beit Vegan 99, Yerushalayim 03.6166340
1091 River Ave., Lakewood NJ 08701 732.370.3344 fax 1.877.Pirchei (732.367.8168)

Self Evaluation Sheets

Discover where you are strong and where you need to work harder on your way to understanding the structures and forms of Hebrew. The Dik Duk book has been edited and rectified many times. This is the first edition of the Dik Duk test. Your input is welcome to help correct, fix, and add information to in order to create a fuller more educational barometer of your command of the Hebrew language. Welcome aboard to a series of comprehensive tests…

I hope you enjoy the self-evaluation!

Note: You van find these 6 sources in the "Artscroll" prayer book, and in most prayer books. If you have these sources , you don't have to download them.

Source materials		Hebrew	English
1.	*Shema Yisrael*	2	3
2.	18 Blessings (*Shemona Esrai*) or *Amida*	4, 6, 8, 10	5, 7, 9, 11
3.	Blessing after eating (*Benching*)	12, 14, 16, 18	13, 15, 17, 19
4.	*Ramban's* 13 Principles of Faith	20	21
5.	Six Constant remembrances	22	23
6.	Ten Commandments	24	25

SELF EVALUATION- SOURCE ONE

The Shema (שמע)

יָחִיד אוֹמֵר: קֵל מֶלֶךְ נֶאֱמָן:

שְׁמַע יִשְׂרָאֵל ה' אֱלֹקֵינוּ, ה' אֶחָד:

בלחש: בָּרוּךְ שֵׁם כְּבוֹד מַלְכוּתוֹ לְעוֹלָם וָעֶד:

First paragraph

וְאָהַבְתָּ אֵת ה' אֱלֹקֶיךָ, בְּכָל לְבָבְךָ וּבְכָל נַפְשְׁךָ וּבְכָל מְאֹדֶךָ: וְהָיוּ הַדְּבָרִים הָאֵלֶּה אֲשֶׁר אָנֹכִי מְצַוְּךָ הַיּוֹם עַל לְבָבֶךָ: וְשִׁנַּנְתָּם לְבָנֶיךָ, וְדִבַּרְתָּ בָּם, בְּשִׁבְתְּךָ בְּבֵיתֶךָ וּבְלֶכְתְּךָ בַדֶּרֶךְ וּבְשָׁכְבְּךָ וּבְקוּמֶךָ: וּקְשַׁרְתָּם לְאוֹת עַל יָדֶךָ, וְהָיוּ לְטֹטָפֹת בֵּין עֵינֶיךָ: וּכְתַבְתָּם עַל מְזֻזוֹת בֵּיתֶךָ וּבִשְׁעָרֶיךָ:

Second paragraph

וְהָיָה אִם שָׁמֹעַ תִּשְׁמְעוּ אֶל מִצְוֹתַי אֲשֶׁר אָנֹכִי מְצַוֶּה אֶתְכֶם הַיּוֹם, לְאַהֲבָה אֶת ה' אֱלֹקֵיכֶם, וּלְעָבְדוֹ בְּכָל לְבַבְכֶם וּבְכָל נַפְשְׁכֶם: וְנָתַתִּי מְטַר אַרְצְכֶם בְּעִתּוֹ יוֹרֶה וּמַלְקוֹשׁ, וְאָסַפְתָּ דְגָנֶךָ וְתִירֹשְׁךָ וְיִצְהָרֶךָ: וְנָתַתִּי עֵשֶׂב בְּשָׂדְךָ לִבְהֶמְתֶּךָ, וְאָכַלְתָּ וְשָׂבָעְתָּ: הִשָּׁמְרוּ לָכֶם פֶּן יִפְתֶּה לְבַבְכֶם, וְסַרְתֶּם וַעֲבַדְתֶּם אֱלֹקִים אֲחֵרִים וְהִשְׁתַּחֲוִיתֶם לָהֶם: וְחָרָה אַף ה' בָּכֶם, וְעָצַר אֶת הַשָּׁמַיִם וְלֹא יִהְיֶה מָטָר וְהָאֲדָמָה לֹא תִתֵּן אֶת יְבוּלָהּ, וַאֲבַדְתֶּם מְהֵרָה מֵעַל הָאָרֶץ הַטֹּבָה אֲשֶׁר ה' נֹתֵן לָכֶם: וְשַׂמְתֶּם אֶת דְּבָרַי אֵלֶּה עַל לְבַבְכֶם וְעַל נַפְשְׁכֶם, וּקְשַׁרְתֶּם אֹתָם לְאוֹת עַל יֶדְכֶם וְהָיוּ לְטוֹטָפֹת בֵּין עֵינֵיכֶם: וְלִמַּדְתֶּם אֹתָם אֶת בְּנֵיכֶם, לְדַבֵּר בָּם, בְּשִׁבְתְּךָ בְּבֵיתֶךָ וּבְלֶכְתְּךָ בַדֶּרֶךְ וּבְשָׁכְבְּךָ וּבְקוּמֶךָ: וּכְתַבְתָּם עַל מְזוּזוֹת בֵּיתֶךָ וּבִשְׁעָרֶיךָ: לְמַעַן יִרְבּוּ יְמֵיכֶם וִימֵי בְנֵיכֶם עַל הָאֲדָמָה אֲשֶׁר נִשְׁבַּע ה' לַאֲבֹתֵיכֶם לָתֵת לָהֶם, כִּימֵי הַשָּׁמַיִם עַל הָאָרֶץ:

Third paragraph

וַיֹּאמֶר ה' אֶל מֹשֶׁה לֵּאמֹר: דַּבֵּר אֶל בְּנֵי יִשְׂרָאֵל, וְאָמַרְתָּ אֲלֵהֶם, וְעָשׂוּ לָהֶם צִיצִת עַל כַּנְפֵי בִגְדֵיהֶם, לְדֹרֹתָם, וְנָתְנוּ עַל צִיצִת הַכָּנָף פְּתִיל תְּכֵלֶת: וְהָיָה לָכֶם לְצִיצִת, וּרְאִיתֶם אֹתוֹ, וּזְכַרְתֶּם אֶת כָּל מִצְוֹת ה', וַעֲשִׂיתֶם אֹתָם. וְלֹא תָתוּרוּ אַחֲרֵי לְבַבְכֶם וְאַחֲרֵי עֵינֵיכֶם, אֲשֶׁר אַתֶּם זֹנִים אַחֲרֵיהֶם: לְמַעַן תִּזְכְּרוּ, וַעֲשִׂיתֶם אֶת כָּל מִצְוֹתָי. וִהְיִיתֶם קְדֹשִׁים לֵאלֹקֵיכֶם: אֲנִי ה' אֱלֹקֵיכֶם, אֲשֶׁר הוֹצֵאתִי אֶתְכֶם מֵאֶרֶץ מִצְרַיִם לִהְיוֹת לָכֶם לֵאלֹקִים. אֲנִי ה' אֱלֹקֵיכֶם: אֱמֶת

English Translation of Shema

The Shema *(שמע)*

If you pray without minyan: G-d, faithful King

Listen, Israel: *Hashem* is our G-d, *Hashem* is One
Softly: Blessed is the Name of His Glorious Kingdom Forever

First paragraph

You shall love *Hashem*, your G-d with all your heart, and with all your soul, and with all your might (or fortune). And let these words which I command you today [be] upon your heart: And you shall teach them diligently to your children: And speak to them when sitting at home, walking on the way, lying down or getting up: And tie them a sign upon your arm, and they shall be totafos [tefillin] between your eyes: And you shall write then upon the doorposts of your house and upon your gates.

Second paragraph

And it will come to pass, if you will diligently listen to my mitzvos which I command you today: to love *Hashem*, your G-d and to serve Him with all your heart, and with all your soul, [then] I will give rain for your land at the right time, the fall and spring rains, so that you may gather in your grain, your wine and your oil: And I will give grass in your field for your cattle, and you will eat and be satisfied. Be careful lest your heart be tempted, and you turn astray and serve other gods and bow to them. Then *Hashem* will act angrily with you. He will restrain the skies and there will be no rain, and the ground will not give its produce, and you will quickly be cast out from the good land, which *Hashem* gives you. Put these words of mine upon your heart and upon your soul, and tie them as a sign upon your arm, and they shall be totafos [tefillin] between your eyes. Teach them to your children, to speak [of] them when sitting at home, walking on the way, lying down or getting up. And you shall write then upon the doorposts of your house and upon your gates. In order that the days and the days of your children will be prolonged upon the land which *Hashem* swore to give to your ancestors, as long as Heaven is above the earth.

Third paragraph

And *Hashem* said to Moshe, saying: Speak to the children [sons] of Israel and say to them that they make for themselves tzitzis [tassels] on the corners of their clothes throughout their generations. And they shall put on the tzitzis of each corner a string of techeiles. This shall be tzitzis for you so that you may see it and remember all the mitzvos of *Hashem* and do them. And you will not stray after your heart and after your eyes which mislead you [away from me], in order that you remember and keep all my mitzvos, and be holy to your G-d, I am *Hashem* your G-d [Elo-him] who brought you out of the land of Egypt to be your G-d. I am *Hashem* your G-d—Emess [True].

SELF EVALUATION – SOURCE TWO

The Shemoneh Esrei (18 blessings)—Amida (שמונה עשרה—עמידה)

בלחש: ה' שְׂפָתַי תִּפְתָּח וּפִי יַגִּיד תְּהִלָּתֶךָ:

1. Father, Chesed

בָּרוּךְ אַתָּה, ה', לקינוּ וֵאלֹקֵי אֲבוֹתֵינוּ. אֱלֹקֵי אַבְרָהָם. אֱלֹקֵי יִצְחָק. וֵאלֹקֵי יַעֲקֹב. הָקֵל הַגָּדוֹל הַגִּבּוֹר וְהַנּוֹרָא קֵל עֶלְיוֹן. גּוֹמֵל חֲסָדִים טוֹבִים. וְקוֹנֵה הַכֹּל. וְזוֹכֵר חַסְדֵי אָבוֹת. וּמֵבִיא גוֹאֵל לִבְנֵי בְנֵיהֶם לְמַעַן שְׁמוֹ בְּאַהֲבָה:

מֶלֶךְ עוֹזֵר וּמוֹשִׁיעַ וּמָגֵן: בָּרוּךְ אַתָּה ה', מָגֵן אַבְרָהָם:

2. Strength, Judgment

אַתָּה גִּבּוֹר לְעוֹלָם, ה', מְחַיֵּה מֵתִים אַתָּה. רַב לְהוֹשִׁיעַ:

בקיץ: מוֹרִיד הַטָּל:
בחורף: מַשִּׁיב הָרוּחַ וּמוֹרִיד הַגֶּשֶׁם:

מְכַלְכֵּל חַיִּים בְּחֶסֶד. מְחַיֶּה מֵתִים בְּרַחֲמִים רַבִּים. סוֹמֵךְ נוֹפְלִים וְרוֹפֵא
חוֹלִים וּמַתִּיר אֲסוּרִים. וּמְקַיֵּם אֱמוּנָתוֹ לִישֵׁנֵי עָפָר. מִי כָמוֹךָ בַּעַל גְּבוּרוֹת
וּמִי דוֹמֶה לָּךְ. מֶלֶךְ מֵמִית וּמְחַיֶּה וּמַצְמִיחַ יְשׁוּעָה:
וְנֶאֱמָן אַתָּה לְהַחֲיוֹת מֵתִים: בָּרוּךְ אַתָּה ה', מְחַיֵּה הַמֵּתִים:

Kedushah

נְקַדֵּשׁ אֶת שִׁמְךָ בָּעוֹלָם, כְּשֵׁם שֶׁמַּקְדִּישִׁים אוֹתוֹ בִּשְׁמֵי מָרוֹם,
כַּכָּתוּב עַל יַד נְבִיאֶךָ. וְקָרָא זֶה אֶל זֶה וְאָמַר:

קו"ח: קָדוֹשׁ. קָדוֹשׁ. קָדוֹשׁ ה' צְבָאוֹת. מְלֹא כָל הָאָרֶץ כְּבוֹדוֹ:

חזן: לְעֻמָּתָם בָּרוּךְ יֹאמֵרוּ:

קו"ח: בָּרוּךְ כְּבוֹד ה' מִמְּקוֹמוֹ:

חזן: וּבְדִבְרֵי קָדְשְׁךָ כָּתוּב לֵאמֹר:

קו"ח: יִמְלֹךְ ה' לְעוֹלָם, אֱלֹקִים צִיּוֹן לְדֹר וָדֹר. הַלְלוּיָהּ:

חזן: לְדוֹר וָדוֹר נַגִּיד גָּדְלֶךָ. וּלְנֵצַח נְצָחִים קְדֻשָּׁתְךָ נַקְדִּישׁ. וְשִׁבְחֲךָ
אֱלֹקֵינוּ מִפִּינוּ לֹא יָמוּשׁ לְעוֹלָם וָעֶד. כִּי
קֵל מֶלֶךְ גָּדוֹל וְקָדוֹשׁ
אָתָּה: בָּרוּךְ אַתָּה ה'. הָקֵל [בעשי"ת הַמֶּלֶךְ] הַקָּדוֹשׁ:

English Translation

The Shemoneh Esrei (18 blessings)—Amida (שמונה עשרה–עמידה)

Softly: My Lord, my lips you will open, and my mouth will declare Your praises.

1. Father, Chesed

Blessed are You,.Lord our God and the God of our fathers, the God of Avraham, the God of Yitzhak, and the God of Ya'akov, the great, the mighty and awesome God, the supreme God, performing beneficial acts of kindness, creating everything, remembering the kindnesses of the fathers, and bringing a redeemer to the sons of their sons with love for the sake of His name.

King, helper, redeemer and protector, blessed are You, Lord, protector of Avraham.

2. Strength, Judgment

You are mighty forever, my Lord. You revive the dead. You constantly rescue.

Summer	You cause the dew to fall.
Winter	You cause the wind to blow, and the rain to fall.

He sustains the living with kindness, revives the dead with great compassion, supports the falling, heals the sick, frees the bound, and establishes His faith of those who sleep in the dust. Who is like you, master of might, and who can be compared to You, King, who brings death, gives life, and causes salvation to blossom? And You can be trusted to revive the dead. Blessed are You, Lord, who revives the dead.

Kedushah

Congregation and then *Chazan*	We will sanctify Your Name in this world, just as they are sanctifying It in Heaven above. As it is written by the hand of Your prophet: And this angel calls to this angel saying:
Congregation	Holy, Holy, Holy is the Lord G-d of Hosts; All the earth is full of His Glory.
Chazan	Those opposite them will say blessed
Congregation	Blessed is the Glory of G-d from His place.
Chazan	And in the words of your Holiness it is written saying:
Congregation	G-o will rule eternally, You G-d of Zion from Generation to Generation
Chazan	From Generation to Generation we will tell of your greatness and for endless eternities Your Holiness will be proclaimed. And your praise Our G-d, from our mouth will not cease eternally, for You are Mighty, King, Great and Holy… Blessed are you the Holy G-d…

Shemoneh Esrei (cont.)

3. Holiness, Beauty

אַתָּה קָדוֹשׁ וְשִׁמְךָ קָדוֹשׁ וּקְדוֹשִׁים בְּכָל יוֹם יְהַלְלוּךָ סֶּלָה. בָּרוּךְ אַתָּה ה'.
הָקֵל [בעשי"ת: הַמֶּלֶךְ] הַקָּדוֹשׁ:

4. Mind, Understanding

אַתָּה חוֹנֵן לְאָדָם דַּעַת. וּמְלַמֵּד לֶאֱנוֹשׁ בִּינָה: חָנֵּנוּ מֵאִתְּךָ דֵּעָה בִּינָה
וְהַשְׂכֵּל: בָּרוּךְ אַתָּה ה', חוֹנֵן הַדָּעַת:

5. Repentance, Tikun

הֲשִׁיבֵנוּ אָבִינוּ לְתוֹרָתֶךָ. וְקָרְבֵנוּ מַלְכֵּנוּ לַעֲבוֹדָתֶךָ וְהַחֲזִירֵנוּ בִּתְשׁוּבָה
שְׁלֵמָה לְפָנֶיךָ. בָּרוּךְ אַתָּה ה', הָרוֹצֶה בִּתְשׁוּבָה:

6. Forgiveness

סְלַח לָנוּ אָבִינוּ, כִּי חָטָאנוּ. מְחַל לָנוּ מַלְכֵּנוּ כִּי פָשָׁעְנוּ. כִּי מוֹחֵל וְסוֹלֵחַ
אָתָּה. בָּרוּךְ אַתָּה ה', חַנוּן הַמַּרְבֶּה לִסְלֹחַ:

7. Redemption

רְאֵה בְעָנְיֵנוּ. וְרִיבָה רִיבֵנוּ. וּגְאָלֵנוּ מְהֵרָה לְמַעַן שְׁמֶךָ. כִּי גּוֹאֵל חָזָק אָתָּה.
בָּרוּךְ אַתָּה ה', גּוֹאֵל יִשְׂרָאֵל:

8. Healing, Physical Well-being

רְפָאֵנוּ, ה', וְנֵרָפֵא. הוֹשִׁיעֵנוּ וְנִוָּשֵׁעָה כִּי תְהִלָּתֵנוּ אָתָּה. וְהַעֲלֵה רְפוּאָה
שְׁלֵמָה לְכָל מַכּוֹתֵינוּ.* כִּי קֵל מֶלֶךְ רוֹפֵא נֶאֱמָן וְרַחֲמָן אָתָּה. בָּרוּךְ אַתָּה
ה'. רוֹפֵא חוֹלֵי עַמּוֹ יִשְׂרָאֵל:

9. Blessing of years, Physical Bounty

בָּרֵךְ עָלֵינוּ, ה' לקינו, אֶת הַשָּׁנָה הַזֹּאת וְאֶת כָּל מִינֵי תְבוּאָתָהּ לְטוֹבָה.
וְתֵן [בקיץ: בְּרָכָה.] [בחורף: טַל וּמָטָר לִבְרָכָה] עַל פְּנֵי הָאֲדָמָה, וְשַׂבְּעֵנוּ
מִטּוּבָהּ. וּבָרֵךְ שְׁנָתֵנוּ כַּשָּׁנִים הַטּוֹבוֹת: בָּרוּךְ אַתָּה ה', מְבָרֵךְ הַשָּׁנִים:

10. Gathering of Exiles

תְּקַע בְּשׁוֹפָר גָּדוֹל לְחֵרוּתֵנוּ. וְשָׂא נֵס לְקַבֵּץ גָּלֻיּוֹתֵינוּ. וְקַבְּצֵנוּ יַחַד מֵאַרְבַּע
כַּנְפוֹת הָאָרֶץ: בָּרוּךְ אַתָּה ה', מְקַבֵּץ נִדְחֵי עַמּוֹ יִשְׂרָאֵל:

---

* Place to add special prayer for one or more who are ill. Say the person full name son of or daughter of their mothers name.

Translation

3. Holiness, Beauty

You are holy, and your name is holy, and holy beings praise You daily. Blessed are You, Lord, the holy God.

4. Mind, Understanding

You graciously give man knowledge, and teach mankind understanding. Grace us with Your knowledge, understanding and intellectual power. Blessed are You, Lord, who graciously gives knowledge.,

5. Repentance, Tikun

Return us, our Father, to Your Torah, and bring us closer, our King, to Your service, and make us return with a complete turning to Your presence. Blessed are You, Lord, who desires repentance.

6. Forgiveness

Forgive us, our Father, because we have sinned. Pardon us, our King, because we have transgressed, and You are He who pardons and forgives. Blessed are You, Lord, the gracious One, who generously forgives.

7. Redemption

See our pain, and fight our fight, and redeem us soon for the sake of Your name. Blessed are You, Lord, Redeemer of Israel.

8. Healing, Physical Well-being

Heal us, Lord, and we will be healed. Save us, and we will be saved, because You are our glory. Bring about a complete healing of our wounds, because You are God, the king, a faithful and merciful healer. Blessed are You, Lord, who heals the sick among His people Israel.

9. Blessing of years, Physical Bounty

Bless for us, Lord, our God, this year, and all its various types of produce for the good. And give (summer) blessing, (winter) dew and rain as a blessing, upon the earth. Satisfy us with your goodness, and bless our years like the good years. Blessed are You, Lord, who blesses the years.

10. Gathering of Exiles

Sound the *shofar* to announce our liberation, raise the banner to gather our exiles, and gather us together from the four corners of the earth. Blessed are You, Lord, who gathers the dispersed of His people, Israel.

Shemoneh Esrei (cont.)

11. Restoration of Justice

הָשִׁיבָה שׁוֹפְטֵינוּ כְּבָרִאשׁוֹנָה. וְיוֹעֲצֵינוּ כְּבַתְּחִלָּה. וְהָסֵר מִמֶּנּוּ יָגוֹן וַאֲנָחָה. וּמְלֹךְ עָלֵינוּ אַתָּה ה' לְבַדְּךָ בְּחֶסֶד וּבְרַחֲמִים. וְצַדְּקֵנוּ בַּמִּשְׁפָּט. בָּרוּךְ אַתָּה ה'. מֶלֶךְ אוֹהֵב צְדָקָה וּמִשְׁפָּט. (בעשי"ת הַמֶּלֶךְ הַמִּשְׁפָּט):

12. Against Heretics Remove Evil

וְלַמַּלְשִׁינִים אַל תְּהִי תִקְוָה. וְכָל הָרִשְׁעָה כְּרֶגַע תֹּאבֵד. וְכָל אוֹיְבֶךָ מְהֵרָה יִכָּרֵתוּ. וְהַזֵּדִים מְהֵרָה תְעַקֵּר וּתְשַׁבֵּר וּתְמַגֵּר וְתַכְנִיעַ בִּמְהֵרָה בְיָמֵינוּ. בָּרוּךְ אַתָּה ה'. שׁוֹבֵר אוֹיְבִים וּמַכְנִיעַ זֵדִים:

13. Blessings to Righteous

עַל הַצַּדִּיקִים וְעַל הַחֲסִידִים. וְעַל זִקְנֵי עַמְּךָ בֵּית יִשְׂרָאֵל. וְעַל פְּלֵיטַת סוֹפְרֵיהֶם. וְעַל גֵּרֵי הַצֶּדֶק וְעָלֵינוּ. יֶהֱמוּ רַחֲמֶיךָ ה' לְקִינוּ. וְתֵן שָׂכָר טוֹב לְכָל הַבּוֹטְחִים בְּשִׁמְךָ בֶּאֱמֶת. וְשִׂים חֶלְקֵנוּ עִמָּהֶם לְעוֹלָם וְלֹא נֵבוֹשׁ כִּי בְךָ בָּטָחְנוּ: בָּרוּךְ אַתָּה ה'. מִשְׁעָן וּמִבְטָח לַצַּדִּיקִים:

14. Rebuild Yerushalaim

וְלִירוּשָׁלַיִם עִירְךָ בְּרַחֲמִים תָּשׁוּב. וְתִשְׁכֹּן בְּתוֹכָהּ כַּאֲשֶׁר דִּבַּרְתָּ. וּבְנֵה אוֹתָהּ בְּקָרוֹב בְּיָמֵינוּ בִּנְיַן עוֹלָם. וְכִסֵּא דָוִד מְהֵרָה לְתוֹכָהּ תָּכִין: בָּרוּךְ אַתָּה ה'. בּוֹנֵה יְרוּשָׁלָיִם:

15. Salvation/Throne of David

אֶת צֶמַח דָּוִד עַבְדְּךָ מְהֵרָה תַצְמִיחַ. וְקַרְנוֹ תָּרוּם בִּישׁוּעָתֶךָ. כִּי לִישׁוּעָתְךָ קִוִּינוּ כָּל הַיּוֹם: בָּרוּךְ אַתָּה ה'. מַצְמִיחַ קֶרֶן יְשׁוּעָה:

16. Acceptance of Prayer

שְׁמַע קוֹלֵנוּ. ה' לְקִינוּ חוּס וְרַחֵם עָלֵינוּ. וְקַבֵּל בְּרַחֲמִים וּבְרָצוֹן אֶת תְּפִלָּתֵנוּ. כִּי קֵל שׁוֹמֵעַ תְּפִלּוֹת וְתַחֲנוּנִים אָתָּה. וּמִלְּפָנֶיךָ מַלְכֵּנוּ. רֵיקָם אַל תְּשִׁיבֵנוּ. כִּי אַתָּה שׁוֹמֵעַ תְּפִלַּת עַמְּךָ יִשְׂרָאֵל בְּרַחֲמִים. בָּרוּךְ אַתָּה ה'. שׁוֹמֵעַ תְּפִלָּה:

17. Temple Service to Express Gratitude

רְצֵה ה' לְקִינוּ בְּעַמְּךָ יִשְׂרָאֵל וּבִתְפִלָּתָם. וְהָשֵׁב אֶת הָעֲבוֹדָה לִדְבִיר בֵּיתֶךָ. וְאִשֵּׁי יִשְׂרָאֵל וּתְפִלָּתָם. בְּאַהֲבָה תְקַבֵּל בְּרָצוֹן. וּתְהִי לְרָצוֹן תָּמִיד עֲבוֹדַת יִשְׂרָאֵל עַמֶּךָ:

Translation

11. Restoration of Justice

Restore our judges as it was at first, and our advisors as it was at the beginning, and remove misery and sighing from us. And rule over us, You alone, Lord, with kindness and mercy, and exonerate us in judgment. Blessed are You, Lord, who loves righteousness and judgment.

12. Against Heretics Remove Evil

Let the informers have no hope, and let all evil disappear in an instant. May all Your enemies be cut off soon, and quickly uproot, break, destroy and humble the evil ones, quickly in our lifetimes. Blessed are You, Lord, who breaks enemies and subdues the evil ones.

13. Blessings to Righteous

Upon the righteous, upon the pious, upon the elders of your people, the house of Israel, upon the remnants of their sages, upon the righteous converts and upon us, may Your mercy be aroused, Lord our God, and give a good reward to all those who truly trust in Your name. Let our portion always be with theirs, and we will not be ashamed, because we trusted in You. Blessed are You, Lord, the support and safe haven of the righteous.

14. Rebuild Yerushalaim

And to Jerusalem, Your city, return with mercy, and abide within it, as you have promised. Build it very soon as an eternal structure, and establish the throne of David within it quickly. Blessed are You, Lord, who builds Jerusalem.

15. Salvation/Throne of David

Let the sapling of David Your servant quickly blossom, and let his power rise up through your salvation, because we have hoped for Your salvation all through the day. Blessed are You, Lord, who makes the glory of salvation blossom.

16. Acceptance of Prayer

Listen to our voice, Lord, our God. Pity us, have mercy on us, and accept our prayer mercifully and willingly, because you are a God who hears prayers and supplications. Do not turn us back empty-handed from in front of You, because You listen to the prayer of Your people Israel with mercy. Blessed are You, Lord, who listens to prayer.

17. Temple Service to Express Gratitude

Be pleased, Lord our God, with Your people Israel and with their prayer, and return the service to the holiest part of Your house. Accept willingly and lovingly the fire-offerings of Israel and their prayer, and let the service of Your people, Israel, be constantly pleasing to You.

Let our eyes gaze upon Your merciful return to Zion. Blessed are You, Lord, who returns His presence to Zion.

Shemoneh Esrei (cont.)

18. Thanksgiving

מוֹדִים אֲנַחְנוּ לָךְ. שָׁאַתָּה הוּא ה' אֱלֹקֵינוּ וֵאלֹקֵי אֲבוֹתֵינוּ לְעוֹלָם וָעֶד. צוּר חַיֵּינוּ. מָגֵן יִשְׁעֵנוּ אַתָּה הוּא לְדוֹר וָדוֹר׃ נוֹדֶה לְּךָ וּנְסַפֵּר תְּהִלָּתֶךָ עַל חַיֵּינוּ הַמְּסוּרִים בְּיָדֶךָ. וְעַל נִשְׁמוֹתֵינוּ הַפְּקוּדוֹת לָךְ. וְעַל נִסֶּיךָ שֶׁבְּכָל יוֹם עִמָּנוּ. וְעַל נִפְלְאוֹתֶיךָ וְטוֹבוֹתֶיךָ שֶׁבְּכָל עֵת. עֶרֶב וָבֹקֶר וְצָהֳרָיִם׃ הַטּוֹב כִּי לֹא כָלוּ רַחֲמֶיךָ. וְהַמְרַחֵם כִּי לֹא תַמּוּ חֲסָדֶיךָ. מֵעוֹלָם קִוִּינוּ לָךְ׃

וְעַל כֻּלָּם יִתְבָּרַךְ וְיִתְרוֹמַם שִׁמְךָ מַלְכֵּנוּ תָּמִיד לְעוֹלָם וָעֶד׃

בעשי"ת׃ וּכְתֹב לְחַיִּים טוֹבִים כָּל בְּנֵי בְרִיתֶךָ׃

וְכֹל הַחַיִּים יוֹדוּךָ סֶּלָה. וִיהַלְלוּ אֶת שִׁמְךָ בֶּאֱמֶת. הָקֵל יְשׁוּעָתֵנוּ וְעֶזְרָתֵנוּ סֶלָה. בָּרוּךְ אַתָּה ה'. הַטּוֹב שִׁמְךָ וּלְךָ נָאֶה לְהוֹדוֹת׃

19. Peace

שִׂים שָׁלוֹם טוֹבָה וּבְרָכָה. חֵן וָחֶסֶד וְרַחֲמִים עָלֵינוּ וְעַל כָּל יִשְׂרָאֵל עַמֶּךָ. בָּרְכֵנוּ אָבִינוּ כֻּלָּנוּ כְּאֶחָד בְּאוֹר פָּנֶיךָ. כִּי בְאוֹר פָּנֶיךָ נָתַתָּ לָנוּ ה' אֱלֹקֵינוּ תּוֹרַת חַיִּים וְאַהֲבַת חֶסֶד. וּצְדָקָה וּבְרָכָה וְרַחֲמִים וְחַיִּים וְשָׁלוֹם. וְטוֹב בְּעֵינֶיךָ לְבָרֵךְ אֶת עַמְּךָ יִשְׂרָאֵל בְּכָל עֵת וּבְכָל שָׁעָה בִּשְׁלוֹמֶךָ׃

בעשי"ת׃ בְּסֵפֶר חַיִּים. בְּרָכָה וְשָׁלוֹם. וּפַרְנָסָה טוֹבָה. נִזָּכֵר וְנִכָּתֵב לְפָנֶיךָ. אֲנַחְנוּ וְכָל עַמְּךָ בֵּית יִשְׂרָאֵל. לְחַיִּים טוֹבִים וּלְשָׁלוֹם׃

בָּרוּךְ אַתָּה ה'. הַמְבָרֵךְ אֶת עַמּוֹ יִשְׂרָאֵל בַּשָּׁלוֹם׃

Prologue

יִהְיוּ לְרָצוֹן אִמְרֵי פִי וְהֶגְיוֹן לִבִּי לְפָנֶיךָ. ה' צוּרִי וְגוֹאֲלִי׃

אֱלֹקַי. נְצֹר לְשׁוֹנִי מֵרָע וּשְׂפָתַי מִדַּבֵּר מִרְמָה. וְלִמְקַלְלַי נַפְשִׁי תִדֹּם. וְנַפְשִׁי כֶּעָפָר לַכֹּל תִּהְיֶה. פְּתַח לִבִּי בְּתוֹרָתֶךָ. וּבְמִצְוֹתֶיךָ תִּרְדֹּף נַפְשִׁי. וְכָל הַחוֹשְׁבִים עָלַי רָעָה. מְהֵרָה הָפֵר עֲצָתָם וְקַלְקֵל מַחֲשַׁבְתָּם׃ עֲשֵׂה לְמַעַן שְׁמֶךָ. עֲשֵׂה לְמַעַן יְמִינֶךָ. עֲשֵׂה לְמַעַן קְדֻשָּׁתֶךָ. עֲשֵׂה לְמַעַן תּוֹרָתֶךָ. לְמַעַן יֵחָלְצוּן יְדִידֶיךָ הוֹשִׁיעָה יְמִינְךָ וַעֲנֵנִי׃ יִהְיוּ לְרָצוֹן אִמְרֵי פִי וְהֶגְיוֹן לִבִּי לְפָנֶיךָ. ה' צוּרִי וְגוֹאֲלִי׃ עֹשֶׂה שָׁלוֹם (בעשי"ת׃ הַשָּׁלוֹם) בִּמְרוֹמָיו. הוּא יַעֲשֶׂה שָׁלוֹם עָלֵינוּ וְעַל כָּל יִשְׂרָאֵל. וְאִמְרוּ אָמֵן׃

Translation

18. Thanksgiving

We thank You because You are the Lord our God and the God of our fathers forever. Rock of our lives, shield of our salvation, You are constant in every generation. We will tell of Your glory and thank You for our lives that are given into Your hand, for our souls which are entrusted to You, for Your miracles that are with us daily, and for Your wonders and Your favors which are which are with us every day: evening, morning and noon. You are the good One--Your mercies never cease. You are the merciful One--Your kindnesses never end. We have always placed our hope in You.

And for everything, our King, may Your name be blessed and uplifted constantly and forever.

And all the living will thank You and they will truly praise Your name, the God of our salvation and our help. Blessed are You, Lord, the good One is Your name, and it is proper to give thanks to You.

19. Peace

Bestow peace, goodness and blessing, grace, kindness and mercy on us and upon all Israel, Your people. Bless us, our Father, all of us together, with the light of Your face, because through the light of Your face, You have given us, Lord, our God, the Torah of life, the love of kindness, and charity, blessing, mercy, life and peace. And it is pleasing to You to bless Your people, Israel, in every season and at every hour, with peace. Blessed are You, Lord, who blesses His people Israel with peace.

Prologue

Let the words of my mouth and the meditation of my heart be acceptable to You, Lord, my Rock and my Redeemer.

My God, keep my tongue from evil and my lips from speaking deceitfully. To those who curse me, let my soul be silent, and let my soul be like dust in relationship to everything. Open my heart to Your Torah, and let my soul chase after Your commandments. Quickly nullify the conspiring of those who wish to do me evil and spoil their plans. Do it for the sake of Your name. Do it for the sake of Your right hand. Do it for the sake of Your holiness. Do it for the sake of Your Torah. Use Your rescuing hand in order to free Your loved ones and answer me. Let the words of my mouth and the meditation of my heart be acceptable to You, Lord, my Rock and my Redeemer.

He who makes peace in His high places, may He make peace for us and for all Israel, and say amen.

SELF EVALUATION – SOURCE THREE

The Blessing after Food (Benching)
(סדר ברכת המזון)

בחול קודם ברכות המזון: (תהילים קלז)

עַל נַהֲרוֹת בָּבֶל שָׁם יָשַׁבְנוּ גַּם בָּכִינוּ, בְּזָכְרֵנוּ אֶת צִיּוֹן: עַל עֲרָבִים בְּתוֹכָהּ, תָּלִינוּ כִּנֹּרוֹתֵינוּ: כִּי שָׁם שְׁאֵלוּנוּ שׁוֹבֵינוּ דִּבְרֵי שִׁיר וְתוֹלָלֵינוּ שִׂמְחָה, שִׁירוּ לָנוּ מִשִּׁיר צִיּוֹן: אֵיךְ נָשִׁיר אֶת שִׁיר ה', עַל אַדְמַת נֵכָר: אִם אֶשְׁכָּחֵךְ יְרוּשָׁלָםִ, תִּשְׁכַּח יְמִינִי: תִּדְבַּק לְשׁוֹנִי לְחִכִּי אִם לֹא אֶזְכְּרֵכִי, אִם לֹא אַעֲלֶה אֶת יְרוּשָׁלַםִ עַל רֹאשׁ שִׂמְחָתִי: זְכֹר ה' לִבְנֵי אֱדוֹם אֵת יוֹם יְרוּשָׁלַםִ, הָאֹמְרִים עָרוּ עָרוּ עַד הַיְסוֹד בָּהּ: בַּת בָּבֶל הַשְּׁדוּדָה, אַשְׁרֵי שֶׁיְשַׁלֶּם לָךְ אֶת גְּמוּלֵךְ שֶׁגָּמַלְתְּ לָנוּ: אַשְׁרֵי שֶׁיֹּאחֵז וְנִפֵּץ אֶת עֹלָלַיִךְ אֶל הַסָּלַע:

בשבת וי"וט וכשאין אומרים תחנון: (תהילים קכו)

שִׁיר הַמַּעֲלוֹת. בְּשׁוּב ה' אֶת שִׁיבַת צִיּוֹן הָיִינוּ כְּחֹלְמִים: אָז יִמָּלֵא שְׂחוֹק פִּינוּ וּלְשׁוֹנֵנוּ רִנָּה. אָז יֹאמְרוּ בַגּוֹיִם הִגְדִּיל ה' לַעֲשׂוֹת עִם אֵלֶּה: הִגְדִּיל ה' לַעֲשׂוֹת עִמָּנוּ. הָיִינוּ שְׂמֵחִים: שׁוּבָה ה' אֶת שְׁבִיתֵנוּ כַּאֲפִיקִים בַּנֶּגֶב: הַזֹּרְעִים בְּדִמְעָה בְּרִנָּה יִקְצֹרוּ: הָלוֹךְ יֵלֵךְ וּבָכֹה נֹשֵׂא מֶשֶׁךְ הַזָּרַע. בֹּא יָבֹא בְרִנָּה. נֹשֵׂא אֲלֻמֹּתָיו:

מים אחרונים חובה קודם ברכת המזון.

המברך אומר:	רַבּוֹתַי. מִיר וֶועלֶן בֶּענְטְשֶׁען (רַבּוֹתַי נְבָרֵךְ):
ועונים המסובים:	יְהִי שֵׁם ה' מְבֹרָךְ מֵעַתָּה וְעַד עוֹלָם:
המזמן חוזר על זה וממשיך:	בִּרְשׁוּת מָרָנָן וְרַבּוֹתַי נְבָרֵךְ: (בעשרה: אֱלֹקֵינוּ) שֶׁאָכַלְנוּ מִשֶּׁלּוֹ:
ואומרים המסובים:	בָּרוּךְ (בעשרה: אֱלֹקֵינוּ) שֶׁאָכַלְנוּ מִשֶּׁלּוֹ וּבְטוּבוֹ חָיִינוּ:
ואח"כ המברך:	בָּרוּךְ (בעשרה: אֱלֹקֵינוּ) שֶׁאָכַלְנוּ מִשֶּׁלּוֹ וּבְטוּבוֹ חָיִינוּ
והמזמן חוזר:	מִי שֶׁלֹּא אָכַל עוֹנֶה: בָּרוּךְ (בעשרה: אֱלֹקֵינוּ) וּמְבוֹרָךְ שְׁמוֹ תָּמִיד לְעוֹלָם וָעֶד:

Blessing 1—Nourishment

בָּרוּךְ אַתָּה ה' אֱלֹקֵינוּ מֶלֶךְ הָעוֹלָם. הַזָּן אֶת הָעוֹלָם כֻּלּוֹ. בְּטוּבוֹ בְּחֵן בְּחֶסֶד וּבְרַחֲמִים. הוּא נוֹתֵן לֶחֶם לְכָל בָּשָׂר. כִּי לְעוֹלָם חַסְדּוֹ. וּבְטוּבוֹ הַגָּדוֹל תָּמִיד לֹא חָסַר לָנוּ וְאַל יֶחְסַר לָנוּ מָזוֹן לְעוֹלָם וָעֶד. בַּעֲבוּר שְׁמוֹ הַגָּדוֹל. כִּי הוּא קֵל זָן וּמְפַרְנֵס לַכֹּל וּמֵטִיב לַכֹּל וּמֵכִין מָזוֹן לְכָל בְּרִיּוֹתָיו אֲשֶׁר בָּרָא. בָּרוּךְ אַתָּה ה'. הַזָּן אֶת הַכֹּל:

Translation

The Blessing after Food (Benching)

תהילים קל"ז

By the river of Babylon there we sat and also we cried, in our remembering Zion. Upon willow in the midst of it we hung our harps. Because there they asked of us, our captures, words of song, and those that shattered us, happiness, sing for us from the song of Zion. How will we sing the song of Hashem on the soil of strangers. If I will forget you Jerusalem my right hand should forget. My tongue will cling to my palate if I do not remember you, if I do not elevate Jerusalem to be my primary source of joy. Remember Hashem the sons of Edom, the day of Jerusalem, the ones who say destroy destroy even until its foundation in it. Daughters of Babylon, the one who is destroyed, praised is the one who's recompense is complete to you, according to how you treated us. Praised is the one who will grasp and shatter suckling infants against the rock.

תהילים קכ"ו

A song of ascents concerning Hashems returning the returnees of zion, we will have been like dreamers. Then our mouth will fill with laughter and our tongue song of exaltation. Then they will say among the nations Hashem has created greatness with these. Hashem has created greatness with us, we were joyous. Hashem return our captivity loke spring in a parched land. The ones who plant with tears with joyous song they will harvest. The one who surely will go along on his way and weeping bearing a measure of seed, surely he will come with joyous song, bearing his sheaves.

מים אחרונים חובה קודם ברכת המזון

(The one leading says):	My friends let us bless.
(All respond):	The name of Hashem it will be blessed from now and eternally.
(The leader continues):	The name of Hashem it will be blessed from now and eternally. With permission our master and our sages, and my friends let us bless since we have eaten from that which is his.
(The other respond):	Blessed is he that we have eaten from what is his and thru his goodness we live.
(The leader continues):	Blessed is the one that we ate from what is his and thru his goodness we live.

Blessing 1—Nourishment

Blessed are you *Hashem*, who nourishes the entire world. In His goodness, as a favor, with kindness, and with mercy, He gives bread to all flesh, both animals and people, because his kindness is endless. And in his goodness we never lacked, and may it be that we will never lack "nourishment"-food, for the sake of His Great Name, because He is the G-d who nourishes, supports, and does good for all. And he prepares food for all His creations, which He has created, as it is said: You open Your Hand and satisfy the wishes of every living thing. Blessed are you *Hashem*,who nourishes all.

Benching (cont.)

Blessing 2—The Land

נוֹדֶה לְּךָ ה' אֱלֹקֵינוּ. עַל שֶׁהִנְחַלְתָּ לַאֲבוֹתֵינוּ אֶרֶץ חֶמְדָּה טוֹבָה וּרְחָבָה. וְעַל שֶׁהוֹצֵאתָנוּ ה' אֱלֹקֵינוּ מֵאֶרֶץ מִצְרַיִם. וּפְדִיתָנוּ מִבֵּית עֲבָדִים. וְעַל בְּרִיתְךָ שֶׁחָתַמְתָּ בִּבְשָׂרֵנוּ. וְעַל תּוֹרָתְךָ שֶׁלִּמַּדְתָּנוּ. וְעַל חֻקֶּיךָ שֶׁהוֹדַעְתָּנוּ. וְעַל חַיִּים חֵן וָחֶסֶד שֶׁחוֹנַנְתָּנוּ. וְעַל אֲכִילַת מָזוֹן שָׁאַתָּה זָן וּמְפַרְנֵס אוֹתָנוּ תָּמִיד. בְּכָל יוֹם וּבְכָל עֵת וּבְכָל שָׁעָה:

בחנוכה ובפורים אומרים:

וְעַל הַנִּסִּים וְעַל הַפֻּרְקָן וְעַל הַגְּבוּרוֹת וְעַל הַתְּשׁוּעוֹת וְעַל הַמִּלְחָמוֹת. שֶׁעָשִׂיתָ לַאֲבוֹתֵינוּ בַּיָּמִים הָהֵם בַּזְּמַן הַזֶּה:

לחנוכה:

בִּימֵי מַתִּתְיָהוּ בֶּן יוֹחָנָן כֹּהֵן גָּדוֹל חַשְׁמוֹנָאִי וּבָנָיו. כְּשֶׁעָמְדָה מַלְכוּת יָוָן הָרְשָׁעָה עַל עַמְּךָ יִשְׂרָאֵל. לְהַשְׁכִּיחָם תּוֹרָתֶךָ וּלְהַעֲבִירָם מֵחֻקֵּי רְצוֹנֶךָ. וְאַתָּה בְּרַחֲמֶיךָ הָרַבִּים. עָמַדְתָּ לָהֶם בְּעֵת צָרָתָם. רַבְתָּ אֶת רִיבָם. דַּנְתָּ אֶת דִּינָם. נָקַמְתָּ אֶת נִקְמָתָם. מָסַרְתָּ גִּבּוֹרִים בְּיַד חַלָּשִׁים. וְרַבִּים בְּיַד מְעַטִּים. וּטְמֵאִים בְּיַד טְהוֹרִים. וּרְשָׁעִים בְּיַד צַדִּיקִים. וְזֵדִים בְּיַד עוֹסְקֵי תוֹרָתֶךָ. וּלְךָ עָשִׂיתָ שֵׁם גָּדוֹל וְקָדוֹשׁ בְּעוֹלָמֶךָ. וּלְעַמְּךָ יִשְׂרָאֵל עָשִׂיתָ תְּשׁוּעָה גְדוֹלָה וּפֻרְקָן כְּהַיּוֹם הַזֶּה. וְאַחַר כַּךְ בָּאוּ בָנֶיךָ לִדְבִיר בֵּיתֶךָ. וּפִנּוּ אֶת הֵיכָלֶךָ. וְטִהֲרוּ אֶת מִקְדָּשֶׁךָ. וְהִדְלִיקוּ נֵרוֹת בְּחַצְרוֹת קָדְשֶׁךָ. וְקָבְעוּ שְׁמוֹנַת יְמֵי חֲנֻכָּה אֵלוּ. לְהוֹדוֹת וּלְהַלֵּל לְשִׁמְךָ הַגָּדוֹל:

לפורים:

בִּימֵי מָרְדְּכַי וְאֶסְתֵּר בְּשׁוּשַׁן הַבִּירָה. כְּשֶׁעָמַד עֲלֵיהֶם הָמָן הָרָשָׁע. בִּקֵּשׁ לְהַשְׁמִיד לַהֲרֹג וּלְאַבֵּד אֶת כָּל הַיְּהוּדִים. מִנַּעַר וְעַד זָקֵן טַף וְנָשִׁים. בְּיוֹם אֶחָד. בִּשְׁלוֹשָׁה עָשָׂר לְחֹדֶשׁ שְׁנֵים עָשָׂר הוּא חֹדֶשׁ אֲדָר וּשְׁלָלָם לָבוֹז. וְאַתָּה בְּרַחֲמֶיךָ הָרַבִּים הֵפַרְתָּ אֶת עֲצָתוֹ. וְקִלְקַלְתָּ אֶת מַחֲשַׁבְתּוֹ. וַהֲשֵׁבוֹתָ לוֹ גְּמוּלוֹ בְּרֹאשׁוֹ. וְתָלוּ אוֹתוֹ וְאֶת בָּנָיו עַל הָעֵץ:

וְעַל הַכֹּל ה' אֱלֹקֵינוּ אֲנַחְנוּ מוֹדִים לָךְ וּמְבָרְכִים אוֹתָךְ. יִתְבָּרַךְ שִׁמְךָ בְּפִי כָּל חַי תָּמִיד לְעוֹלָם וָעֶד: כַּכָּתוּב: וְאָכַלְתָּ וְשָׂבָעְתָּ וּבֵרַכְתָּ אֶת ה' אֱלֹקֶיךָ עַל הָאָרֶץ הַטֹּבָה אֲשֶׁר נָתַן לָךְ: בָּרוּךְ אַתָּה ה'. עַל הָאָרֶץ וְעַל הַמָּזוֹן:

Translation

Blessing 2—The Land

We thank You, *Hashem* our G-d that You have given the heritage *Eretz Yisrael*, to our forefathers a land that is desired which is good and which is wide. And that You took us out, *Hashem* our G-d, from the land of Egypt, and saved us from the house of slavery. And for your statutes [laws] which you made known to us, and for life, grace, and the kindness which you do for us, and for eating of the food with which You nourish us, and which You provide for us constantly every day, and at set times of the day, and in every hour.

For Chanukah and Purim
(And) for the miracles, and for freeing us, and for the mighty acts, and for saving us, and for the wars (that You fought for us) – that You did for our forefathers in those days at this time:

For Chanukah
In the days of *Mattisyahu* the son of *Yochanan*, the *Kohen Gadol* (the high Priest), The *Hasmonean* and his sons, the wicked kingdom of Greece ruled over You nation *Yisroel*, to make them forget Your Torah, and to lead them away from Your *mitzvos*. You, in Your great kindness, stood by them in their time of trouble. You fought their fights judged their judgments; took revenge for them. You handed the strong to the weak. You let a few people conquer many people. You handed those who are *tamei* into the hands of those who are *tahor*. You made the wicked people lose to the righteous people. You handed people who did sins to people who keep Your Torah. For Yourself, You made a great and holy name in Your World. On this day, You saved and freed us. Afterwards, your children came to the holiest place of Your house, and they cleaned out Your *Beis Hamikdash* (Temple). They lit lights in the courtyard of Your *Beis Hamikdash*, and they set down for all time that these eight days of *Chanukah* should be used for giving thanks and praises to Your great name.

For Purim
In the days of *Mordechai* and Esther, in the capital of *Shushan*, when the wicked *Haman* stood up against them (the Jewish people), he wanted to destroy, to kill and to wide out all the Jewish people, infants and women, on one day, (that is), on the thirteenth day pf the twelfth month which is *Adar*. But You, in Your great kindness, caused this bad advise to fail, and did not allow his evil ideas to happen. You caused all his plans to backfire. They hanged him and his sons on the gallows.

And for everything, *Hashem* our G-d, we thank You and bless You, may Your name be blessed in the mouth of all living creatures, always for all time. For it is written: "And you should eat and be satisfied, and bless *Hashem*, your G-d, for the good land which He gives you." Blessed are you *Hashem* for the land and for the food.

Benching (cont.)

Blessing 3—Jerusalem

רַחֵם נָא ה' אֱלֹקֵינוּ עַל יִשְׂרָאֵל עַמֶּךָ. וְעַל יְרוּשָׁלַיִם עִירֶךָ. וְעַל צִיּוֹן מִשְׁכַּן
כְּבוֹדֶךָ. וְעַל מַלְכוּת בֵּית דָּוִד מְשִׁיחֶךָ. וְעַל הַבַּיִת הַגָּדוֹל וְהַקָּדוֹשׁ שֶׁנִּקְרָא
שִׁמְךָ עָלָיו: אֱלֹקֵינוּ. אָבִינוּ. רְעֵנוּ זוּנֵנוּ פַּרְנְסֵנוּ וְכַלְכְּלֵנוּ וְהַרְוִיחֵנוּ. וְהַרְוַח
לָנוּ ה' אֱלֹקֵינוּ מְהֵרָה מִכָּל צָרוֹתֵינוּ. וְנָא אַל תַּצְרִיכֵנוּ ה' אֱלֹקֵינוּ לֹא לִידֵי
מַתְּנַת בָּשָׂר וָדָם וְלֹא לִידֵי הַלְוָאָתָם. כִּי אִם לְיָדְךָ הַמְּלֵאָה. הַפְּתוּחָה.
הַקְּדוֹשָׁה וְהָרְחָבָה. שֶׁלֹּא נֵבוֹשׁ וְלֹא נִכָּלֵם לְעוֹלָם וָעֶד:

לשבת:

רְצֵה וְהַחֲלִיצֵנוּ ה' אֱלֹקֵינוּ בְּמִצְוֹתֶיךָ וּבְמִצְוַת יוֹם הַשְּׁבִיעִי הַשַּׁבָּת הַגָּדוֹל
וְהַקָּדוֹשׁ הַזֶּה כִּי יוֹם זֶה גָּדוֹל וְקָדוֹשׁ הוּא לְפָנֶיךָ לִשְׁבָּת בּוֹ וְלָנוּחַ בּוֹ
בְּאַהֲבָה כְּמִצְוַת רְצוֹנֶךָ וּבִרְצוֹנְךָ הָנִיחַ לָנוּ ה' אֱלֹקֵינוּ שֶׁלֹּא תְהֵא צָרָה
וְדְאָגָה וְיָגוֹן וַאֲנָחָה בְּיוֹם מְנוּחָתֵנוּ וְהַרְאֵנוּ ה' אֱלֹקֵינוּ בְּנֶחָמַת צִיּוֹן עִירֶךָ
וּבְבִנְיַן יְרוּשָׁלַיִם עִיר קָדְשֶׁךָ כִּי אַתָּה הוּא בַּעַל הַיְשׁוּעוֹת וּבַעַל הַנֶּחָמוֹת:

לראש חדש, ליום טוב ולחול המועד:

אֱלֹקֵינוּ וֵאלֹקֵי אֲבוֹתֵינוּ יַעֲלֶה וְיָבֹא וְיַגִּיעַ וְיֵרָאֶה וְיֵרָצֶה וְיִשָּׁמַע וְיִפָּקֵד
וְיִזָּכֵר זִכְרוֹנֵנוּ וּפִקְדוֹנֵנוּ וְזִכְרוֹן אֲבוֹתֵינוּ וְזִכְרוֹן מָשִׁיחַ בֶּן דָּוִד עַבְדֶּךָ
וְזִכְרוֹן יְרוּשָׁלַיִם עִיר קָדְשֶׁךָ וְזִכְרוֹן כָּל עַמְּךָ בֵּית יִשְׂרָאֵל לְפָנֶיךָ לִפְלֵיטָה
לְטוֹבָה לְחֵן וּלְחֶסֶד וּלְרַחֲמִים לְחַיִּים טוֹבִים וּלְשָׁלוֹם בְּיוֹם

לר"ח:	רֹאשׁ הַחֹדֶשׁ הַזֶּה:	לפסח:	חַג הַמַּצּוֹת הַזֶּה:
לשבועות:	חַג הַשָּׁבֻעוֹת הַזֶּה:	לסוכות:	חַג הַסֻּכּוֹת הַזֶּה:
לשמ"ע ולש"ת:	שְׁמִינִי חַג הָעֲצֶרֶת הַזֶּה:	לר"ה:	בְּיוֹם הַזִּכָּרוֹן הַזֶּה:
	ילדים האוכלים ביו"כ:	הַכִּפּוּרִים הַזֶּה.	

זָכְרֵנוּ ה' אֱלֹקֵינוּ בּוֹ לְטוֹבָה וּפָקְדֵנוּ בּוֹ לִבְרָכָה וְהוֹשִׁיעֵנוּ בּוֹ לְחַיִּים
טוֹבִים. וּבִדְבַר יְשׁוּעָה וְרַחֲמִים חוּס וְחָנֵּנוּ וְרַחֵם עָלֵינוּ וְהוֹשִׁיעֵנוּ כִּי אֵלֶיךָ
עֵינֵינוּ כִּי קֵל חַנּוּן וְרַחוּם אָתָּה:

וּבְנֵה יְרוּשָׁלַיִם עִיר הַקֹּדֶשׁ בִּמְהֵרָה בְיָמֵינוּ. בָּרוּךְ אַתָּה ה'. בּוֹנֵה בְרַחֲמָיו
יְרוּשָׁלָיִם: אָמֵן:

Translation

Blessing 3—Jerusalem

Have mercy, *Hashem* our G-d, on us and on Israel, Your people and on Jerusalem, Your city and on Zion, the place of your Honor and on the kingdom of the house of David, Your anointed one, and on the *Beis Hamikdash* the great and holy house that your name is called on it. Our Lord our Father, watch over us, feed us, give us clothing and a place to live, support us regularly, and give us enough to live comfortably. And quickly give us relief from all our troubles, that we should not be embarrasses or ashamed forever.

Prayer added on *Shabbos*

Be pleases and save us, *Hashem* our G-d, by Your commandments and by the mitzvah of the seventh day-which is the mitzvah of keeping *Shabbos*, because this is a great day before you to rest and be calm on it, with love, as a commandment of your will. Let it be your will to allow us to rest, *Hashem* our G-d, so that there will be no trouble or sadness, or mourning on our day of rest, and let us see, *Hashem* our G-d, Zion your city, being comforted and Jerusalem, the city of Your holiness being rebuilt because You are the One who has power to help and the ability to give comfort.

Prayer added on the New Moon, New Year and Festivals

Our G-d and the G-d of our fathers, let (our pleas) go up, and come (to You) and reach (You), and be seen (by You), and be accepted, and be heard, and be counted, and be remembered, a reminder and thoughts of us, and a reminder of our forefathers, a reminder of Jerusalem, your city, and a reminder of *Moshiach,* the son of David, Your servant, and a reminder of all Your people the house of Israel (should come) before You. (Think of us) to save us, for our good, as a favor, and as a kindness, and with mercy, for a good life, and for peace, on this day of:

On Rosh *Chodesh*	Rosh *Chodesh* (the New Moon)	On Pesach	The festival of Matzos
On *Shavous*	The festival of *Shavous*	On Sukkos	The festival of Sukkos
On Rosh *Hashana*	Remembrance		
On *Shemini Atzeres* and *Simhas* Torah	The festival of *Shemini Atzeres*		

To have mercy onus on this day and to save us. Remember us *Hashem* our G-d, on this day, for good, and think of us for blessing, and save us for a good life. And having to do with saving and mercy, have pity on us and show us favor, and have compassion and mercy on us and save us. Because our eyes (look) to You, because You are G-d, King and merciful.

And may You build Jerusalem, the holy city, quickly in our days. Blessed are You *Hashem*, who builds Jerusalem. Amen

Benching (cont.)

Blessing 4—Goodness of Hashem

בָּרוּךְ אַתָּה ה' אֱלֹקֵינוּ מֶלֶךְ הָעוֹלָם. הָאֵל. אָבִינוּ. מַלְכֵּנוּ. אַדִּירֵנוּ. בּוֹרְאֵנוּ.
גּוֹאֲלֵנוּ. יוֹצְרֵנוּ. קְדוֹשֵׁנוּ קְדוֹשׁ יַעֲקֹב. רוֹעֵנוּ רוֹעֵה יִשְׂרָאֵל. הַמֶּלֶךְ הַטּוֹב
וְהַמֵּטִיב לַכֹּל. שֶׁבְּכָל יוֹם וָיוֹם הוּא הֵטִיב הוּא מֵטִיב הוּא יֵיטִיב לָנוּ. הוּא
גְמָלָנוּ הוּא גוֹמְלֵנוּ הוּא יִגְמְלֵנוּ לָעַד לְחֵן וּלְחֶסֶד וּלְרַחֲמִים וּלְרֶוַח. הַצָּלָה
וְהַצְלָחָה. בְּרָכָה וִישׁוּעָה. נֶחָמָה. פַּרְנָסָה וְכַלְכָּלָה. וְרַחֲמִים וְחַיִּים וְשָׁלוֹם
וְכָל טוֹב. וּמִכָּל טוֹב לְעוֹלָם אַל יְחַסְּרֵנוּ:

[End of Benching from the Torah]

Rabbinic Benching

הָרַחֲמָן הוּא יִמְלֹךְ עָלֵינוּ לְעוֹלָם וָעֶד:
הָרַחֲמָן הוּא יִתְבָּרַךְ בַּשָּׁמַיִם וּבָאָרֶץ:
הָרַחֲמָן הוּא יִשְׁתַּבַּח לְדוֹר דּוֹרִים. וְיִתְפָּאַר בָּנוּ לָעַד וּלְנֵצַח נְצָחִים.
וְיִתְהַדַּר בָּנוּ לָעַד וּלְעוֹלְמֵי עוֹלָמִים: הָרַחֲמָן הוּא יְפַרְנְסֵנוּ בְּכָבוֹד:
הָרַחֲמָן הוּא יִשְׁבֹּר עֻלֵּנוּ מֵעַל צַוָּארֵנוּ וְהוּא יוֹלִיכֵנוּ קוֹמְמִיּוּת לְאַרְצֵנוּ:
הָרַחֲמָן הוּא יִשְׁלַח לָנוּ בְּרָכָה מְרֻבָּה בַּבַּיִת הַזֶּה וְעַל שֻׁלְחָן זֶה שֶׁאָכַלְנוּ עָלָיו:
הָרַחֲמָן הוּא יִשְׁלַח לָנוּ אֶת אֵלִיָּהוּ הַנָּבִיא זָכוּר לַטּוֹב וִיבַשֶּׂר לָנוּ בְּשׂוֹרוֹת
טוֹבוֹת יְשׁוּעוֹת וְנֶחָמוֹת:
הָרַחֲמָן הוּא יְבָרֵךְ אֶת (אָבִי מוֹרִי) בַּעַל הַבַּיִת הַזֶּה וְאֶת (אִמִּי מוֹרָתִי)
בַּעֲלַת הַבַּיִת הַזֶּה. אוֹתָם וְאֶת בֵּיתָם וְאֶת זַרְעָם וְאֶת כָּל אֲשֶׁר לָהֶם.
(וְאִם סָמוּךְ עַל שֻׁלְחָן עַצְמוֹ יֹאמַר) אוֹתִי (וְאָבִי וְאִמִּי) וְאִשְׁתִּי וְזַרְעִי וְאֶת כָּל
אֲשֶׁר לִי), אוֹתָנוּ וְאֶת כָּל אֲשֶׁר לָנוּ. כְּמוֹ שֶׁנִּתְבָּרְכוּ אֲבוֹתֵינוּ אַבְרָהָם יִצְחָק
שְׁלֵמָה. וְנֹאמַר אָמֵן: וְיַעֲקֹב בַּכֹּל מִכֹּל כֹּל. כֵּן יְבָרֵךְ כֻּלָּנוּ יַחַד בִּבְרָכָה

בַּמָּרוֹם יְלַמְּדוּ עֲלֵיהֶם וְעָלֵינוּ זְכוּת שֶׁתְּהֵא לְמִשְׁמֶרֶת שָׁלוֹם. וְנִשָּׂא בְרָכָה
מֵאֵת ה'. וּצְדָקָה מֵאֱלֹקֵי יִשְׁעֵנוּ. וְנִמְצָא חֵן וְשֵׂכֶל טוֹב בְּעֵינֵי אֱלֹקִים וְאָדָם:

הָרַחֲמָן הוּא יְזַכֵּנוּ לִימוֹת הַמָּשִׁיחַ וּלְחַיֵּי הָעוֹלָם הַבָּא:
(בְּחוֹל: מַגְדִּיל בַּיּוֹם שֶׁיֵּשׁ בּוֹ מוּסָף אוֹמֵר: מִגְדּוֹל) יְשׁוּעוֹת מַלְכּוֹ וְעֹשֶׂה חֶסֶד
לִמְשִׁיחוֹ לְדָוִד וּלְזַרְעוֹ עַד עוֹלָם: עֹשֶׂה שָׁלוֹם בִּמְרוֹמָיו הוּא יַעֲשֶׂה שָׁלוֹם
עָלֵינוּ וְעַל כָּל יִשְׂרָאֵל וְאִמְרוּ אָמֵן:

יְראוּ אֶת ה' קְדוֹשָׁיו כִּי אֵין מַחְסוֹר לִירֵאָיו: כְּפִירִים רָשׁוּ וְרָעֵבוּ וְדֹרְשֵׁי
ה' לֹא יַחְסְרוּ כָל טוֹב: הוֹדוּ לַה' כִּי טוֹב כִּי לְעוֹלָם חַסְדּוֹ: פּוֹתֵחַ אֶת יָדֶךָ
וּמַשְׂבִּיעַ לְכָל חַי רָצוֹן: בָּרוּךְ הַגֶּבֶר אֲשֶׁר יִבְטַח בַּה' וְהָיָה ה' מִבְטַחוֹ: נַעַר
הָיִיתִי גַּם זָקַנְתִּי וְלֹא רָאִיתִי צַדִּיק נֶעֱזָב וְזַרְעוֹ מְבַקֶּשׁ לָחֶם: ה' עֹז לְעַמּוֹ
יִתֵּן ה' יְבָרֵךְ אֶת עַמּוֹ בַשָּׁלוֹם:

Translation

Blessing 4—Goodness of Hashem

Blessed are You, *Hashem* our G-d, king of the universe the Almighty, our Father, our King, our strong one, our Creator, our Redeemer, our maker, our Holy One, the Holy One of Yaakov. Our shepherd, the shepherd of Israel, the king who is good and who does good to all, that each and every day He did good; He does good; He will do good for all of us. He did kindness for us; He does kindness for us; He will do kindness for us forever. With grace, and with kindness, and with mercy, and for relief [from our troubles], by saving [us], and success, blessing, and help, comfort, a way of making a living, taking care of our needs, and mercy, and life, and peace, and all good, and from all good things may He never deprive us.

[End of Benching from the Torah]

Rabbinic Benching

May the Merciful One reign over us forever.

May the Merciful One be blessed in heaven and on earth.

May the Merciful One be praised in every generation and through us may *Hashem* be glorified forever, until the end of time.

May the Merciful One support us with honor.

May the Merciful One break the yoke of oppression from our necks and He will deliver us with dignity and pride to our land.

May the Merciful One send great blessing to this house, and on this table where we have eaten.

May the Merciful One send us Elijah the prophet, remembered for good, and may He bring us good news of saving us and comforting us.

May the Merciful One bless (my father, my teacher) the man of this house, and (my mother, my teacher) the woman of this house, them, and their home, and their children, and everything that is theirs. Ours and all that is ours; just as our forefathers Abraham, Isaac, and Jacob were blessed, with all, from all, and in every way. So may He bless us together with a complete blessing. May this be His will, and let us say Amen.

In Heaven, may they and we, be deserving that we should have the protection of peace. And may we get a Blessing from *Hashem*, and kindness form the G-d who saves us. And let us find favor and understanding in the eyes of G-d and man.

May the Merciful One let us be deserving of the days of *Moshiach* and the life of the world to come.

On weekdays: He who makes great the salvations of His King

On *Shabbos*, Festivals and Rosh *Chodesh*: He who is a tower of salvations to His King

And does kind ness to His *Moshiach* , to Dovid and His children forever. He who makes peace in His heavens, may He make peace for us and for all Israel, and say Amen.

Let His holy people fear G-d, because those who fear Him will not lack anything. Young lions may suffer hunger, but those who look to *Hashem* will not lack any good thing. Give thanks to *Hashem* because He is good; His kindness is forever. You open Your hand, and provide the needs of living things. Blessed is the man who trusts in *Hashem*, and *Hashem* will be His trust. I was young and now I am old, and I have never seen *Hashem* forget about a righteous man, or his children having to beg for bread. *Hashem* will give His people strength, *Hashem* will bless his nation with peace.

SELF EVALUATION – SOURCE FOUR

Rambam's 13 Principles of Faith

שלשה עשר עקרים על יסוד דברי הרמב"ם ז"ל, בהקדמתו לפה"מ לפרק חלק

א   אֲנִי מַאֲמִין בֶּאֱמוּנָה שְׁלֵמָה. שֶׁהַבּוֹרֵא יִתְבָּרַךְ שְׁמוֹ הוּא בּוֹרֵא וּמַנְהִיג לְכָל הַבְּרוּאִים. וְהוּא לְבַדּוֹ עָשָׂה וְעוֹשֶׂה וְיַעֲשֶׂה לְכָל הַמַּעֲשִׂים:

ב   אֲנִי מַאֲמִין בֶּאֱמוּנָה שְׁלֵמָה. שֶׁהַבּוֹרֵא יִתְבָּרַךְ שְׁמוֹ הוּא יָחִיד וְאֵין יְחִידוּת כָּמוֹהוּ בְּשׁוּם פָּנִים. וְהוּא לְבַדּוֹ אֱלֹקֵינוּ. הָיָה הֹוֶה וְיִהְיֶה:

ג   אֲנִי מַאֲמִין בֶּאֱמוּנָה שְׁלֵמָה. שֶׁהַבּוֹרֵא יִתְבָּרַךְ שְׁמוֹ אֵינוֹ גוּף. וְלֹא יַשִּׂיגוּהוּ מַשִּׂיגֵי הַגּוּף. וְאֵין לוֹ שׁוּם דִּמְיוֹן כְּלָל:

ד   אֲנִי מַאֲמִין בֶּאֱמוּנָה שְׁלֵמָה. שֶׁהַבּוֹרֵא יִתְבָּרַךְ שְׁמוֹ הוּא רִאשׁוֹן וְהוּא אַחֲרוֹן:

ה   אֲנִי מַאֲמִין בֶּאֱמוּנָה שְׁלֵמָה. שֶׁהַבּוֹרֵא יִתְבָּרַךְ שְׁמוֹ לוֹ לְבַדּוֹ רָאוּי לְהִתְפַּלֵּל. וְאֵין לְזוּלָתוֹ רָאוּי לְהִתְפַּלֵּל:

ו   אֲנִי מַאֲמִין בֶּאֱמוּנָה שְׁלֵמָה. שֶׁכָּל דִּבְרֵי נְבִיאִים אֱמֶת:

ז   אֲנִי מַאֲמִין בֶּאֱמוּנָה שְׁלֵמָה. שֶׁנְּבוּאַת מֹשֶׁה רַבֵּנוּ עָלָיו הַשָּׁלוֹם הָיְתָה אֲמִתִּית. וְשֶׁהוּא הָיָה אָב לַנְּבִיאִים. לַקּוֹדְמִים לְפָנָיו וְלַבָּאִים אַחֲרָיו:

ח   אֲנִי מַאֲמִין בֶּאֱמוּנָה שְׁלֵמָה. שֶׁכָּל הַתּוֹרָה הַמְּצוּיָה עַתָּה בְּיָדֵינוּ הִיא הַנְּתוּנָה לְמֹשֶׁה רַבֵּנוּ עָלָיו הַשָּׁלוֹם:

ט   אֲנִי מַאֲמִין בֶּאֱמוּנָה שְׁלֵמָה. שֶׁזֹּאת הַתּוֹרָה לֹא תְהֵא מֻחְלֶפֶת וְלֹא תְהֵא תוֹרָה אַחֶרֶת מֵאֵת הַבּוֹרֵא יִתְבָּרַךְ שְׁמוֹ:

י   אֲנִי מַאֲמִין בֶּאֱמוּנָה שְׁלֵמָה. שֶׁהַבּוֹרֵא יִתְבָּרַךְ שְׁמוֹ יוֹדֵעַ כָּל מַעֲשֵׂה בְנֵי אָדָם וְכָל מַחְשְׁבוֹתָם. שֶׁנֶּאֱמַר: הַיֹּצֵר יַחַד לִבָּם הַמֵּבִין אֶל כָּל מַעֲשֵׂיהֶם:

יא   אֲנִי מַאֲמִין בֶּאֱמוּנָה שְׁלֵמָה. שֶׁהַבּוֹרֵא יִתְבָּרַךְ שְׁמוֹ גּוֹמֵל טוֹב לְמִי שֶׁיִּשְׁמוֹר מִצְוֹתָיו וּמַעֲנִישׁ לְמִי שֶׁיַּעֲבוֹר עַל מִצְוֹתָיו:

יב   אֲנִי מַאֲמִין בֶּאֱמוּנָה שְׁלֵמָה. בְּבִיאַת הַמָּשִׁיחַ. וְאַף עַל פִּי שֶׁיִּתְמַהְמֵהַּ. עִם כָּל זֶה אֲחַכֶּה לּוֹ בְּכָל יוֹם שֶׁיָּבוֹא:

יג   אֲנִי מַאֲמִין בֶּאֱמוּנָה שְׁלֵמָה. שֶׁתִּהְיֶה תְּחִיַּת הַמֵּתִים בְּעֵת שֶׁתַּעֲלֶה רָצוֹן מֵאֵת הַבּוֹרֵא יִתְבָּרַךְ שְׁמוֹ וְיִתְעַלֶּה זִכְרוֹ לָעַד וּלְנֵצַח נְצָחִים:

Translation

Rambam's 13 Principles of Faith

1. I believe with complete faith, that the Creator, blessed is His name, is the creator and guide of all creations, and He alone made, makes, and will make every thing.

2. I believe with complete faith, that the Creator, blessed is His name, is One, and there is no unity that is in any way like His, and that He alone is our God who was, is, and will be.

3. I believe with complete faith, that the Creator, blessed is His name, is not a physical body. He cannot be affected by physical events, and absolutely nothing resembles Him.

4. I believe with complete faith, that the Creator, blessed is His name, is the first and He is the last.

5. I believe with complete faith, that it is proper to pray only to the Creator, blessed is His name, and it is improper to pray to any other than Him.

6. I believe with complete faith, that all the words of the prophets are true.

7. I believe with complete faith, that the prophecy of Moses, our teacher, may peace be upon him, was true, and that he was the greatest of all prophets—both those who came before him and those who came after him.

8. I believe with complete faith, that the whole Torah that we now have, is the same one that was given to Moses, our teacher, may peace be upon him.

9. I believe with complete faith, that this Torah will never be replaced, and there will never be another Torah from the Creator, blessed is His name.

10. I believe with complete faith, that the Creator, blessed is His name, knows all the actions and all the thoughts of people, as it is written, "He forms their hearts whole (?). He understands their actions".

11. I believe with complete faith, that the Creator, blessed is His name, rewards those who keep His commandments, and punishes those who do not keep His commandments.

12. I believe with complete faith, in the coming of the messiah, and even though he may be delayed, nonetheless, I will wait every day for his arrival.

13. I believe with complete faith, that the dead will come to life at a time that is pleasing to the Creator, may His name be blessed, and may our awareness of Him be elevated forever and ever.

SELF EVALUATION – SOURCE FIVE

Six Constant remembrances
שֵׁשׁ זְכִירוֹת

[א] זכירת יציאת מצרים

לְמַעַן תִּזְכֹּר אֶת יוֹם צֵאתְךָ מֵאֶרֶץ מִצְרַיִם כֹּל יְמֵי חַיֶּיךָ:

[ב] זכירת מעמד הר סיני

רַק הִשָּׁמֶר לְךָ וּשְׁמֹר נַפְשְׁךָ מְאֹד. פֶּן תִּשְׁכַּח אֶת הַדְּבָרִים אֲשֶׁר רָאוּ
עֵינֶיךָ. וּפֶן יָסוּרוּ מִלְּבָבְךָ כֹּל יְמֵי חַיֶּיךָ. וְהוֹדַעְתָּם לְבָנֶיךָ וְלִבְנֵי בָנֶיךָ: יוֹם
אֲשֶׁר עָמַדְתָּ לִפְנֵי ה' אֱלֹקֶיךָ בְּחֹרֵב.

[ג] זכירת מעשה עמלק ומחייתו

זָכוֹר אֵת אֲשֶׁר עָשָׂה לְךָ עֲמָלֵק בַּדֶּרֶךְ בְּצֵאתְכֶם מִמִּצְרָיִם: אֲשֶׁר קָרְךָ
בַּדֶּרֶךְ וַיְזַנֵּב בְּךָ כָּל הַנֶּחֱשָׁלִים אַחֲרֶיךָ. וְאַתָּה עָיֵף וְיָגֵעַ. וְלֹא יָרֵא אֱלֹקִים :
וְהָיָה בְּהָנִיחַ ה' אֱלֹקֶיךָ לְךָ מִכָּל אֹיְבֶיךָ מִסָּבִיב בָּאָרֶץ אֲשֶׁר ה' אֱלֹקֶיךָ נֹתֵן
לְךָ נַחֲלָה לְרִשְׁתָּהּ. תִּמְחֶה אֶת זֵכֶר עֲמָלֵק מִתַּחַת הַשָּׁמָיִם. לֹא תִּשְׁכָּח:

[ד] זכירת מעשי העגל

זְכֹר אַל תִּשְׁכַּח אֵת אֲשֶׁר הִקְצַפְתָּ אֶת ה' אֱלֹקֶיךָ בַּמִּדְבָּר:

[ה] זכירת מעשה מרים

זָכוֹר אֵת אֲשֶׁר עָשָׂה ה' אֱלֹקֶיךָ לְמִרְיָם בַּדֶּרֶךְ בְּצֵאתְכֶם מִמִּצְרָיִם:

[ו] זכירת שבת

זָכוֹר אֶת יוֹם הַשַּׁבָּת לְקַדְּשׁוֹ:

Translation

Six Constant Remembrances

[1] Remembrance of the exodus from Egypt

...In order that you will remember the day you went out from the land of Egypt all the days of your life.

[2] Remembrance of receiving the Torah on mount Sinai

Only be careful for yourself, and watch yourself closely, so as not to forget the things that your eyes saw, or perhaps they will be removed from your heart all the days of your life; and make it known to your children and the children of your children about them—the day that you stood in front of the Lord your God at *Horev*.

[3] Remembrance of *Amalek's* attack

Remember what *Amalek* did to you on the way as you left from Egypt, where he happened to meet you on the road, and he cut down in you all of the weak who trailed behind you; and you were tired and worn out, and he didn't fear God. Therefore, it will be when the Lord your God lets you rest from all your enemies who surround you, in the land that the Lord your God is giving you as an inheritance to keep it, you will erase the memory of *Amalek* from under the skies—you will not forget.

[4] Remembrance of the golden calf

Remember—you should not forget—that you angered the Lord your God in the wilderness.

[5] Remembrance of Miriam

Remember that which the Lord your God did to Miriam on the way as you left from Egypt.

[6] Remembrance of *Shabbos*

Remember the day of *Shabbos* to sanctify it.

SELF EVALUATION – SOURCE SIX

Ten Commandments

וַיְדַבֵּר אֱלֹהִים אֵת כָּל הַדְּבָרִים הָאֵלֶּה לֵאמֹר:

[א] אָנֹכִי יְהֹוָה אֱלֹהֶיךָ אֲשֶׁר הוֹצֵאתִיךָ מֵאֶרֶץ מִצְרַיִם מִבֵּית עֲבָדִים:

[ב] לֹא יִהְיֶה לְךָ אֱלֹהִים אֲחֵרִים עַל פָּנָי: לֹא תַעֲשֶׂה לְךָ פֶסֶל וְכָל תְּמוּנָה אֲשֶׁר בַּשָּׁמַיִם מִמַּעַל וַאֲשֶׁר בָּאָרֶץ מִתָּחַת וַאֲשֶׁר בַּמַּיִם מִתַּחַת לָאָרֶץ: לֹא תִשְׁתַּחֲוֶה לָהֶם וְלֹא תָעָבְדֵם כִּי אָנֹכִי יְהֹוָה אֱלֹהֶיךָ אֵל קַנָּא פֹּקֵד עֲוֹן אָבֹת עַל בָּנִים עַל שִׁלֵּשִׁים וְעַל רִבֵּעִים לְשֹׂנְאָי: וְעֹשֶׂה חֶסֶד לַאֲלָפִים לְאֹהֲבַי וּלְשֹׁמְרֵי מִצְוֹתָי:

[ג] לֹא תִשָּׂא אֶת שֵׁם יְהֹוָה אֱלֹהֶיךָ לַשָּׁוְא כִּי לֹא יְנַקֶּה יְהֹוָה אֵת אֲשֶׁר יִשָּׂא אֶת שְׁמוֹ לַשָּׁוְא:

[ד] זָכוֹר אֶת יוֹם הַשַּׁבָּת לְקַדְּשׁוֹ: שֵׁשֶׁת יָמִים תַּעֲבֹד וְעָשִׂיתָ כָּל מְלַאכְתֶּךָ: וְיוֹם הַשְּׁבִיעִי שַׁבָּת לַיהֹוָה אֱלֹהֶיךָ לֹא תַעֲשֶׂה כָל מְלָאכָה אַתָּה וּבִנְךָ וּבִתֶּךָ עַבְדְּךָ וַאֲמָתְךָ וּבְהֶמְתֶּךָ וְגֵרְךָ אֲשֶׁר בִּשְׁעָרֶיךָ: כִּי שֵׁשֶׁת יָמִים עָשָׂה יְהֹוָה אֶת הַשָּׁמַיִם וְאֶת הָאָרֶץ אֶת הַיָּם וְאֶת כָּל אֲשֶׁר בָּם וַיָּנַח בַּיּוֹם הַשְּׁבִיעִי עַל כֵּן בֵּרַךְ יְהֹוָה אֶת יוֹם הַשַּׁבָּת וַיְקַדְּשֵׁהוּ:

[ה] כַּבֵּד אֶת אָבִיךָ וְאֶת אִמֶּךָ לְמַעַן יַאֲרִכוּן יָמֶיךָ עַל הָאֲדָמָה אֲשֶׁר יְהֹוָה אֱלֹהֶיךָ נֹתֵן לָךְ:

[ו] לֹא תִרְצָח

[ז] לֹא תִנְאָף

[ח] לֹא תִגְנֹב

[ט]לֹא תַעֲנֶה בְרֵעֲךָ עֵד שָׁקֶר:

[י] לֹא תַחְמֹד בֵּית רֵעֶךָ לֹא תַחְמֹד אֵשֶׁת רֵעֶךָ וְעַבְדּוֹ וַאֲמָתוֹ וְשׁוֹרוֹ וַחֲמֹרוֹ וְכֹל אֲשֶׁר לְרֵעֶךָ:

Translation

The Ten Commandments

[1] I am the Lord, your God, who took you out of the land of Egypt, from the house of slaves. You will have no gods other than me.

[2] Do not make a sculpture for yourself, nor a picture of anything that is in the skies above, or on the earth below, or in the water that is below the earth. Do not bow down to them and do not serve them because I, the Lord your God, am an impassioned God, applying the sins of the fathers to the sons until the third and fourth generations for those who hate me. And doing kindness for a thousand generations for those who love me and keep my commandments.

[3] Do not use the name of the Lord your God for no purpose, because the Lord will not pardon someone who uses His name for no purpose.

[4] Remember the Sabbath day, to make it holy. You will toil for six days, and you will do all your work. The seventh day is a Sabbath for the Lord your God. Do not do any work—neither you, your son, your daughter, your slave, your maidservant, nor your stranger within your gates. Because in six days the Lord made the skies and the earth, the sea and everything that is in them, and on the seventh day he rested; therefore the Lord blessed the Sabbath day and made it holy. [5] Honor your father and your mother, in order to lengthen your days upon the land that the Lord your God is giving you.

[6] Do not murder.

[7] Do not commit adultery.

[8] Do not steal.

[9] Do not testify falsely against your fellow man.

[10] Do not desire your fellow man's wife, his slave, his maidservant, his ox, his donkey, nor anything that belongs to your fellow man.

Part 1: (Based on part 1 of, Dik Duk Buk)

* Not technically a vowel

Questions   Answers

1. In the 6 remembrances #2 "Receiving the Torah from Mount Sinai", how many *Dagesh Kals* are there? (pg. 23)

2. In the 6 remembrances #6 "To remember the Sabbath", how many *Beged Kefet Dagesh Kals* are there? (pg. 23)

3. In the 6 remembrances #3 "*Amalek*". (pg. 23)

    a. How many *Dagesh Kals* are there?

    b. How many *Dagesh chazaks* are there?

4. In the 6 remembrances #4 "The Golden Calf..." (pg. 23)

    a. How many Long vowels are there?

    b. How many Short vowels are there?

    c. How many *chataf** Vowels are there?

5. In the 6 remembrances #6 "Remember the Sabbath..." (pg. 23)

    a. How many Long vowels are there?

    b. How many Short vowels are there?

    c. How many *chataf** Vowels are there?

6. In the 6 remembrances #5 "...Miriam..." (pg. 23)

    a. How many Long vowels are there?

    b. How many Short vowels are there?

    c. How many *chataf** Vowels are there?

7. In the 13 Principles of Faith #2 "Creators Uniqueness...": (pg. 21)

    a. How many *sheva na* are there?

    b. How many *sheva nach* are there?

    c. How many *chataf sheva na* are there?

    d. How many *chataf sheva nach* are there?

8. In the last of the 13 Principles of Faith #13 "Resurrection of dead": (pg. 21)

    a. How many *sheva na* are there?

    b. How many *sheva nach* are there?

    c. How many *chataf sheva na* are there?

    d. How many *chataf sheva nach* are there?

Note: There is a difference of opinion as to whether the ל in ולנצח is a *na* or *nach*.

9. In the forth of the 10 commandments (שבת): (pg. 25)

    a. How many *sheva na* are there? _____

    b. How many *sheva nach* are *there*? _____

    c. How many *chataf sheva na* are there? _____

    d. How many *chataf sheva nach* are there? _____

Note: There is a difference of opinion as to whether the ב in ובהמתך is a *na* or *nach*.

10. In the fifth blessing of the *Shemona Esrai* (Repentance): (pg. 7)

    a. How many *sheva* na are there? _____

    b. How many *sheva nach* are there? _____

    c. How many *chataf sheva na* are there? _____

    d. How many chataf *sheva nach* are there? _____

11. How many syllables are there in these words of the *Shemona Esrai*:

    a. הֲשִׁיבֵנוּ _____

    b. בְּעָנְיֵנוּ _____

    c. וּגְאָלֵנוּ _____

    d. סוֹפְרֵיהֶם _____

    e. לְעוֹלָם _____

    f. הַצַּדִּיקִים _____

    g. תְּפִלּוֹת _____

    h. גְּבוּרוֹת _____

    i. וְהַחֲזִירֵנוּ _____

12. In the first blessing of *Bentching* (nourishment), how many letters have a *dagesh chazak*? (pg. 13)

13. What are the first and last words, in the first blessing of *Bentching*, with a *dagesh chazak*? (pg. 13)

    first: _____

    Last: _____

14. How many *dagesh chazaks* are there in the forth blessing of *Bentching* (goodness of Hashem)[i.e. form ברוך through יהסרנו] (pg. 19)

15. Find at least four words in the *Bentching* that have both a *dagesh chazak* and a *dagesh ka*l in them. (pg. 13-19)

    1. _____

    2. _____

    3. _____

    4. _____

Part 2: (Nouns, Pronouns, Adjectives)

Questions   Answers

1. In the first paragraph of *Shema* find a definite noun with its demonstrative adjective. (pg. 3)

2. In the first blessing of the *Shemona Esrei* find a masculine plural noun with its adjective? (pg. 5)

3. In the second blessing of the *Shemona Esrei* find a plural noun and its adjective? (pg. 5)

4. In the fifth blessing of the *Shemona Esrei* (Repentance) find a feminine singular noun and adjective. (pg. 7)

5. In blessing seven of *Shemona Esrei* (Redemption) find a masculine singular noun and its adjective. (pg. 7)

6. In the ninth blessing of *Shemona Esrei* (Prosperity) find: (pg. 7)

    a. Feminine singular definite noun and adjective.

    b. A definite feminine singular noun.

    c. An irregular feminine plural noun and adjective.

7. In the last blessing of the *Shemona Esrei* (*Sim Shalom*), find: (pg. 11)

    a. Three masculine nouns or adjectives.

    b. Three feminine nouns or adjectives.

    c. Two feminine singular construct nouns.

    d. One masculine singular construct noun.

8. In the first blessing of the *Shemona Esrei*, find: (pg. 5)

    a. Masculine plural construct.

    b. Masculine singular construct

9. In the second blessing of *Bentching* (*Eretz Yisrael*), find: An irregular feminine noun and its adjectives. (pg. 15)

10. In the introduction to the 10 commandments, before the first command, find a masculine singular construct noun followed by a masculine plural noun that is also a demonstrative pronoun. (pg. 25)

11. In the forth of the 10 commandments, identify: (pg. 25)

    a. Second person singular possessive on a masculine plural noun

    b. Two construct nouns.

    c. What is the long form of a. above?

12. In the second of the 10 commandments, find: (pg. 25)

    a. Three objects of preposition.

    b. How many possessive pronoun endings are there?

13. In the forth of the 10 commandments (pg. 25) _____

    a. How many second person masculine singular possessive pronoun ending are there?

    b. Find a third person plural direct object of a proposition. _____

14. In the last of the 10 commandments how many possessive pronoun ending are there? (pg. 25)

    a. In second person masculine singular _____

    b. In third person masculine singular _____

15. In the first blessing of *Bircas Hamazon*: (pg. 13)

    a. There are 2 forms of a third person masculine singular possessive pronoun: find at least 1 of each. _____

    b. Find a first person plural object of a preposition. _____

16. In the second blessing of *Bircas Hamazon* (pg. 15)

    a. How many Possessive pronoun endings are there? _____

    b. How many objects of preposition are there? (including also direct object preposition) _____

    c. Find a feminine singular construct? _____

17. In the first paragraph of the *Kriyat Shema*: (pg. 3)

    a. How many possessive pronoun endings? _____

    b. Objects of prepositions? _____

    c. Feminine plural construct? _____

    d. Is the feminine plural construct definite or indefinite? _____

18. In the second Paragraph of *Kriyat Shema*: (pg. 3)

    a. Find First person possessive pronoun of a plural feminine noun. _____

    b. How many second person plural possessive pronouns? _____

    c. How many second person singular possessive pronouns? _____

    d. How many objects of prepositions? _____

    e. How many direct object of verbs are connected directly to the verb? _____

    f. How many direct object of verbs are separate word? _____

19. In the third paragraph of *Kriyat Shema*: (pg. 3)

    a. How many objects of preposition are there?

    b. Find two masculine plural constructs.   _____

    c. A possessive third person Masculine plural, on a feminine plural noun   _____

    d. Find 3 direct objects of verbs with the direct object being a separate word?   _____

     _____

20. In the third paragraph of *Kriyat Shema* (צִיצִת): (pg. 3)

    a. How many second person plural possessive pronouns are there?

    b. How many second person plural objects of preposition are there?   _____

    c. How many third person masculine objects of preposition are there?   _____

    d. How many third person possessive pronoun plural masculine?   _____

     _____

Part 3: (Verbs, Dropping letter, Command form)

Questions   Answers

1. In the first and second paragraph of the *Kriyat Shema* how many:
   (pg. 3)

   a. Second person plural masculine verbs?   _____

   b. Second person singular verbs, with masculine plural direct
      object?   _____

   c. List the first and last word of a.   _____

   d. List the middle two words in b.   _____

2. In the first paragraph of the *Shema* find: (pg. 3)

   a. Second person past tense masculine *pa'al* verb with the
      reversing ו.   _____

   b. Present tense pe-al *binyan* masculine with second person
      singular masculine direct object.   _____

   c. Second person past singular with masculine plural direct
      object in the *pi'el* and in *pa'al*.   _____

3. In the first paragraph of the *Shema* find: (pg. 3)

   a. A ל-ה root in third person plural past in *pa'al binyan*, with
      reversing vav.   _____

   b. A second person past tense *pi'el* with reversing vav.   _____

4. In the second paragraph of the *Shema* find: (pg. 3)

   a. An active future plural verb proceeded by absolute *makor*.   _____

   b. What *binyan* is the active verb in a?   _____

   c. A *pi'el* masculine singular present with its subject
      pronoun.   _____

   d. What is the root of מְצַוֶּה?   _____

5. In the second paragraph of *Shema* find: (pg. 3)

   a. An infinitive with third person singular direct object.   _____

   b. How many second person, singular past in *pa'al*.   _____

   c. How many first person, past tense verbs.   _____

6. In the second paragraph of the *Shema* find a *niph'al binyan*
   command form. (pg. 3)

                                                                     _____

7. In the second paragraph of the *Shema* how many forms of the נתן can you find? Explain & Define each. (pg. 3)

_____

_____

_____

_____

_____

7a. What is the subject of the word תִּתֵּן?

8. In the second paragraph of the *Shema* find: (pg. 3)

    a. A verb in the *niph'al binyan*.

    b. Find A *hispa'el binyan* with a reverse תש. Ignore the reversing vav. What is the root?

    c. Find a *pa'al binyan* with a *patach* (-) under the first root letter in the past

    d. What is the root.

    e. How many Direct Objects of transitive verb?

    f. Direct Object connected to verb.

    g. Direct Object as a separate word.

9. In the third paragraph of the *Shema* find: (pg. 3)

    a. *Pi'el* command form singular.

    b. A ל-ה *pa'al* in third person past tense with reversing vav.

    c. A ל-ה second person past plural In the paal

    d. A פ"י first person in *hiph'il binyan*

    e. A infinitive of ל"ה in *pa'al binyan*

    f. How many direct objects of verbs (as separate words) list them?

    g. How many object of prepositions (indirect objects) list them?

    h. How many verb infinitives?

    i. Find 2 second person masculine plural future tense words, without reversing vav.

10. In the first blessing of *Bircas Hamazon* (nourishment) find:
    (pg. 13)

    a. Find 2 ע"ו verbs in present tense. _____

    b. *Find a noun with a possessive pronoun ending with the same root shoresh as an active verb in past tense. *Ignore reversing ו's / * Based on two letter shoresh _____

    c. What Is the root of the verb to nourish? _____

    d. Find the definite noun form of this toot using its present tense _____

    e. Find a noun form (food/nourishment) _____

    f. A root letter verb expressed in the passed & future _____

11. In the second blessing of *Birchas Hamazon* (ברכת הארץ) Find:
    (pg. 15)

    a. Present tense singular verb of פ"י shoresh _____

    b. What is the root of שֶׁהִנְחַלְתָּ? What is its construct? _____

    c. Second person singular *Hiph'il* of a פ"י with a Direct object. _____

    d. A ל"ה *pa'al binyan* 2nd person past with direct object 1st person plural. _____

    e. What is the *binyan* & tense of שֶׁלִּמַּדְתָּנוּ? _____

    f. What is the נו at the end? _____

    g. What is the root of שֶׁהוֹדַעְתָּנוּ? _____

    h. What is the relative *makor* and infinitive _____

    i. What is the root of מוֹדִים: What's its form? _____

12. In the third blessing of the Benching find: (pg. 17)

    a. A *niph'al* singular verb (with prefix) _____

    b. What is the subject of the verb? _____

    c. At the end of the third *Bracha* what is the form of:

       i. נֵבוֹש _____

       ii. נִכָּלֵם _____

13. In the forth Blessing of the *Birchas Hamazon*: (pg. 19)

    a. Find a definite noun with possessive pronoun ending and followed by a masculine singular construct. _____

    b. How many masculine singular constructs? _____

    c. How many first person plural possessive pronoun endings? _____

    d. Find a singular noun followed by 2 definite adjectives.

14. In the 4ᵗʰ blessing of benching: (pg. 19)

   a. List the 3 verbs formed from the root טוב and the root גמל

   b. What are the *binyan* or each?

   c. List in the order from past to present to future

15. In the 4ᵗʰ blessing of benching, What is: (pg. 19)

   a. The *Binyan* of the word יחסרנו?

   b. Tense/ Number/ Gender?

   c. What is the נו suffix?

   d. Translate יחסרנו

16. In the 2ⁿᵈ rabbinic הָרַחֲמָן (in the rabbinic blessings): (pg. 19)

   a. What is the *binyan* of יתברך?

   b. What is the root of ישתבח?

   c. What kind of *dagesh* is in the ת?

   d. What kind of *dagesh* in the ב

17. In the blessing בַּמָּרוֹם   (pg. 19)

   a. What is the *Binyan* of וְנִשָּׂא?

   b. Tense/Person/Number

18. What is the difference between: מַגְדִּיל That we say during the week, and מִגְדּוֹל That we say on *Shabbos*? (pg. 19)

19. In the last paragraph of *Benching*: (pg. 19)

   a. What are root and form יִרְאוּ?

   b. What are its *binyan*, gender and tense?

   c. What is וּמַשְׂבִּיעַ?

20. In last paragraph of benching, translate: (pg. 19)

   a. הָיִיתִי

   b. זָקַנְתִּי

   c. רָאִיתִי

21. The word נֶעֱזָב, what is: (pg. 19)

   a. Root

   b. Binyan

   c. Gender

   d. Tense

   e. Number

Part 4: (Questions from Shemone Esrei)

Questions   Answers

1. In the introduction to ש"ע: (pg. 5)

   a. What is the root word of שְׂפָתַי?   _____

   b. What is the suffix   _____

   c. Is the root word שְׂפָתַיִם madculine or feminine?   _____

2. In the introduction to shemoneh esrei (ש"יע), what is the: (pg. 5)

   a. *Binyan* of יַגִּיד?   _____

   b. Root of יַגִּיד?   _____

3. In the first blessing of ש"ע (pg. 5)

   a. What is the root of וּמֵבִיא?   _____

   b. What is the *binyan* and Tense?   _____

   c. Find a פ"י root in *hiph'il binyan*.   _____

4. In the Second Blessing: (pg. 5)

   a. Find an infinitive *hiph'il* of a פ"י   _____

   b. What are the root and *binyan* of the word מֵשִׁיב?   _____

   c. What is the root of מוֹרִיד?   _____

   d. What is מְכַלְכֵּל   _____

   e. What is the root of מְכַלְכֵּל?   _____

   f. What is the root of מַתִּיר?   _____

   g. Find 3 present tense verbs in a row.   _____

   h. What *binyan* are they.   _____

   i. Find an infinite form of *hiph'il* word   _____

5. In the third blessing קדושה (holiness) of ש"ע find: (pg. 7)

   a. Masculine plural future tense verb with second person
      direct object.   _____

   b. What is the root of the verb יְהַלְלוּךָ   _____

6. In the eighth blessing (for healing): (pg. 7) _____

    a. What are the *binyan*, person and number of וְנֵרָפֵא?

    b. What are the form, *binyan* and category of הוֹשִׁיעֵנוּ? _____

    c. What are the *binyan*, number, person and root of ונושעה? _____

    d. What are the *binyan* and root of וְהַעֲלֵה? _____

    e. What is a tripe construct noun series? _____

7. In the ninth blessing for a good year: (pg. 7) _____

    a. What is כַּשָּׁנִים הַטּוֹבוֹת

    b. What is שָׁנִים, masculine or feminine? _____

    c. Is it definite or indefinite? _____

8. In the tenth blessing of ש"ע – "Gathering Exiles" What is the _____
difference between: מְקַבֵּץ and וְקַבְּצֵנוּ? (pg. 7)

9. In the eleventh blessing "Restoration of Justice": (pg. 9) _____

    a. What are the form, category and *binyan* of הֵשִׁיבָה?

    b. What is the root of וְיוֹעֲצֵינוּ? _____

    c. What is the form of וְיוֹעֲצֵינוּ? _____

10. In the twelfth blessing "Against Heretics": (pg. 9) _____

    a. וְלַמַּלְשִׁינִים = what is *binyan* and tense?

    b. What is the root? _____

    c. Is the ל prefix a preposition or sign of the infinitive? _____

    d. What is the root of the word איביך? _____

11. In the thirteenth blessing of ש"ע (righteousness) Translate _____
בָטָחְנוּ (pg. 9)

12. In blessing for Jerusalem, blessing 14: (pg. 9) _____

    a. What Are the 2 possible translation of תָּשׁוּב, of the word
out of context?

    b. Find a Pi-al *binyan* second person masculine verb past _____
tense.

    c. Find a third person masculine singular *pi'el*.

    d. What is the root of תָּכִין? _____

13. In the first blessing (Reign of David) Find: (pg. 9) _____

    a. A ל"ה verb.

    b. What is the root? _____

    c. What is its *binyan*? _____

    d. How many *hiph'il* words are there? _____

14. In the seventeenth Blessing רצה: (pg. 9)

    a. What is the root of וְתֶחֱזֶינָה?

    b. What is the *binyan*

    c. Person/Gender/Number

    d. What is the subject of וְתֶחֱזֶינָה?

15. In the eighteenth blessing "Gratitude": (pg. 11)

    a. What is the root of מוֹדִים?

    b. What is the form of מוֹדִים (*binyan*)?

    c. What is the *binyan* of נוֹדֶה?

    d. What is the *binyan* Tense/Person of נְסַפֵּר?

    e. Find at least 2 verbs in *hispa'el*?

    f. What is the root of the *hispa'el* of each of these words?

Part 5: (Test of general princiopals and forms)

This is the final review test question. It is in itself a test on how well you have learned the principles and patterns of *Loshen HaKodesh*.

Question	Page
1. Name and identify the 5 long, and 5 short vowels.	
2. Can you name the 6 *begged kefet* letters?	_____
3. Can you state the primary rule of the *sheva* נָח?	_____
4. Can you state the 5 rules of the *sheva* נָע?	_____
5. Do you know the rules of the *dagesh hazak*	_____
6. Can you identify the letters and vowels that function as direct objects or possessive pronouns or objects of prepositions	_____
7. Can you say out using the root פעל the 7 *binyanim* in the past, present and future?	_____
8. Can you state the sign of person gender number and tense in every verb, 12 in the past, 12 in the future, and 4 in the present tense?	_____

Answers

Part 1

1. 7

2. 0

3. a. 11
   b. 10

4. a. 6
   b. 10
   c. 2

5. a. 5
   b. 4
   c. 0

6. a. 10
   b. 10 **
   c. 2

7. a. 8
   b. 2
   c. 2
   d. 2

8. a. 5 or 6 (they argue if וּלְנֵצַח is נע or נח)
   b. 3 or 4
   c. 1
   d. 3

9. a. 13
   b. 6
   c. 3
   d. 3

10. a. 6
    b. 3
    c. 1
    d. 2

11. a. 3
    b. 3
    c. 4
    d. 3
    e. 2
    f. 4
    g. 2
    h. 2
    i. 4

12. 11

13. first word אַתָּה
    last word: הַכֹּל

14. 11

15. a. בַּשָּׁמַיִם
    b. כֻּלוֹ
    c. שֶׁלִּמַּדְתָּנוּ
    d. כַּכָּתוּב
    e. יִשְׁתַּבַּח
    f. בַּבַּיִת
    g. שֶׁנִּתְבָּרְכוּ
    h. בַּכֹּל

**(the 2 expreassion of לכל are in)

Answers

Part 2

1. הַדְּבָרִים הָאֵלֶּה

2. חֲסָדִים טוֹבִים

3. בְּרַחֲמִים רַבִּים

4. בִּתְשׁוּבָה שְׁלֵמָה

5. גּוֹאֵל חָזָק

6. a. הַשָּׁנָה הַזֹּאת
   b. הָאֲדָמָה
   c. כַּשָּׁנִים הַטּוֹבוֹת

7. a. חֵן, וְחֶסֶד, וְרַחֲמִים
   b. טוֹבָה, וּבְרָכָה, וּצְדָקָה
   c. תּוֹרַת חַיִּים, וְאַהֲבַת חֶסֶד
   d. יִשְׂרָאֵל עַמֶּךָ

8. a. חַסְדֵי אָבוֹת
   b. מָגֵן אַבְרָהָם

9. אֶרֶץ חֶמְדָּה, טוֹבָה, וּרְחָבָה

10. כָּל הַדְּבָרִים הָאֵלֶּה

11. a. אֱלֹקֶיךָ
    b. מִבֵּית עֲבָדִים, מֵאֶרֶץ מִצְרַיִם, יוֹם הַשַּׁבָּת, כָּל מְלַאכְתֶּךָ
    c. אֱלֹקִים שֶׁלְּךָ

12. a. לְךָ, לְךָ, לָהֶם
    b. 5 (מִצְוֹתַי, לְאֹהֲבַי, לְשֹׂנְאָי, אֱלֹקֶיךָ, פָּנָי)

13. a. 9
    b. בָּם

14. a. 3
    b. 4

15. a. type 1:
    בְּטוּבוֹ = in his goodness,
    חַסְדּוֹ = his kindness,
    שְׁמוֹ = his name,
    type 2:
    בְּרִיּוֹתָיו = with all his creation
    b. לָנוּ

16. a. 10
    b. 5
    c. אֲכִילַת מָזוֹן

17. a. 15
    b. 1
    c. מְזוּזוֹת בֵּיתֶךָ
    d. Definite

18. a. מִצְוֹתַי
    b. 13
    c. 11
    d. 6
    e. 2
    f. 3

19. a. 4
    b. בְּנֵי יִשְׂרָאֵל, כַּנְפֵי בִגְדֵיהֶם
    c. לְדֹרֹתָם
    d. הוֹצֵאתִי אֶתְכֶם, רְאִיתֶם אוֹתוֹ, וַעֲשִׂיתֶם אֹתָם

20. a. 5
    b. 2
    c. 3
    d. 1

Answers

Part 3

1. a. 8
   b. 4
   c. first: תִּשְׁמְעוּ last: וְלִמַּדְתֶּם
   d. Middle 2: וּכְתַבְתָּם, וּקְשַׁרְתָּם

2. a. וְאָהַבְתָּ
   a. מְצַוְּךָ
   b. pi-el = וְשִׁנַּנְתָּם,
   pa-al = וּכְתַבְתָּם or וּקְשַׁרְתָּם

3. a. וְהָיוּ
   b. וְדִבַּרְתָּ

4. a. שָׁמֹעַ תִּשְׁמְעוּ
   b. pa-al future 3rd plural
   c. אָנֹכִי מְצַוֶּה
   d. צוה

5. a. וּלְעָבְדוֹ
   b. 4 (one with a direct object)
   c. 2

6. הִשָּׁמְרוּ

7. a. וְנָתַתִּי: pa-al banyan past tense 1st person with reversing. And I will give.
   b. נֹתֵן: present tense pa-al banyan singular masculine. He / it is giving.
   c. לָתֵת: pa-al infinitive. To give.
   d. תִּתֵּן: pa-al banyan 3rd person future feminine singular. She / it will give.

7a. הָאֲדָמָה

8. a. נִשְׁבַּע
   b. וְהִשְׁתַּחֲוִיתֶם/שׁחה
   c. וְשַׂמְתֶּם
   d. שׂים
   e. 4
   f. וּלְעָבְדוֹ / וּכְתַבְתָּם
   g. אֶתְכֶם/אוֹתָם

9. a. דִּבֶּר
   b. וְעָשׂוּ
   c. וּרְאִיתֶם
   d. הוֹצֵאתִי
   e. לִהְיוֹת

f. אֶתְכֶם, אוֹתָם, אוֹתוֹ
g. אֲלֵיהֶם לָהֶם לָכֶם
h. לִהְיוֹת, לֵאמֹר
i. תָּתוּרוּ תִזְכְּרוּ

10. a. וּמֵטִיב, וּמֵכִין
    b. וּבְרִיּוֹתָיו – for all his creatures.
    בָּרָא – he has created.
    c. זוּן
    d. הַזָּן
    e. מָזוֹן
    f. יֶחְסַר חָסַר

11. a. נוֹדֶה (ידה root)
    b. נחל, hiphal 2nd person past.
    c. שֶׁהוֹצֵאתָנוּ (יצא root)
    d. וּפְדִיתָנוּ
    e. piel 2nd person past
    f. direct object: us
    g. ידע
    h. לָדַעַת דַּעַת
    i. ידה, present masculine plural hiphal

12. a. שֶׁנִּקְרָא
    b. שְׁמָךְ
    c. 1. future פָּעַל banyan, root בוש, 1st person plural
    2. niphal future, 1st person plural, root כלם

13. a. אֱלֹקֵינוּ מֶלֶךְ הָעוֹלָם
    b. 3
    c. 9
    d. הַמֶּלֶךְ הַטּוֹב וְהַמֵּטִיב

14. a. טוב is in the hiphal גמל in paal
    b. past הֵטִיב, present מֵטִיב, future יֵטִיב
    c. past גְּמָלָנוּ, present גּוֹמְלֵנוּ, future יִגְמְלֵנוּ

15. a. pi-al
    b. future / singular / masculine
    c. direct object 1st person plural
    d. he will deprive us.

Answers

Part 3

16. a. hit-paal
    b. שׁבח
    c. dagesh kal
    d. dagesh hazak

17. a. pa-al
    b. future / 1ˢᵗ person / plural

18. hiphal present tense singular – he who makes great.
noun form of root גדל – he who is a tower

19. a. ירא / command / 2ⁿᵈ person / masculine plural
    b. pa-al/masculine/future
    c. hiph-il / present / masculine / singular

20. a. I was
    b. I aged
    c. I saw

21. עזב / niphal / singular / masculine / present

Answers

Part 4

1. a. שָׂפָה
   b. possessive pronoun 1st person
   c. plural, feminine (body part)

2. a. hiphal
   b. נגד

3. a. בוא
   b. hiphal/present
   c. וּמוֹשִׁיעַ

4. a. לְהוֹשִׁיעַ
   b. נשב / hiphal binyan
   c. ירד
   d. pi-al present tense
   e. כלכל
   f. נתר
   g. מֵמִית / וּמְחַיֶּה / וּמַצְמִיחַ
   h. hiphal / pi-el / hiphal
   i. לְהַחֲיוֹת

5. a. יְהַלְלוּךָ
   b. הלל

6. a. niphal / 1st / plural
   b. hiphal command, ישע root פ״י
      direct object us
   c. niphal/ 1st person
      plural/future tense
   d. hiphal/ עלה
   e. רוֹפֵא חוֹלֵי עַמּוֹ יִשְׂרָאֵל

7. a. a plural noun & adjective
   b. feminine
   c. definite

8. a. pi-al banyan with direct
      object in command form
   b. present tense pi-al as noun or
      verb

9. a. command/ע״י/hiphal
   b. יעץ
   c. compound noun masculine,
      singular noun/ 1st person pl.

   p.p.

10. a. present tense hiphal binyan
       plural, with a ל prefix
    b. לשנ
    c. proposition
    d. איב

11. we trusted

12. a. you will return, she will
       return
    b. דִּבַּרְתָּ
    c. וְכִסֵּא
    d. כון

13. a. קָוִינוּ
    b. קוה
    c. pi-el
    d. 2

14. a. חזה
    b. pa-al
    c. 2nd or 3rd / feminine / plural
    d. עֵינֵינוּ

15. a. ידה
    b. hip-il pl. masculine present
    c. hif-il פ״י 1st person future
       plural
    d. pi-el/future/first
    e. יִתְבָּרַךְ וְיִתְרוֹמַם
    f. ברך/רמם or רום

HEBREW GRAMMAR
Students' Quick Reference Guide

---

[1] The Alphabetical Hebrew Letters

ת ש ר ק צ פ ף ע ס נ ן מ ם ל כ ך י ט ח ז ו ה ד ג ב א	Print
(script letters)	Script
ת ש ר ק צ ף פ ע ס נ ן מ ם ל כ ך י ט ח ז ו ה ד ג ב א	Rashi

---

[2] Direct Object

Singular

	Verb Object suffix	As a separate word	
Me	נִי or יִ	אוֹתִי	1st person
You *m*	ךָ	אוֹתְךָ	2nd person
You *f*	ךְ	אוֹתָךְ	2nd person
Him *m*	ו, יו, הו, נּ	אוֹתוֹ	3rd person
Her *f*	הָ	אוֹתָהּ	3rd person

Plural

Us	נוּ	אוֹתָנוּ	1st person
you *m*	כֶם	אֶתְכֶם	2nd person
You *f*	כֶן	אֶתְכֶן	2nd person
Them *m*	ם	אוֹתָם	3rd person
Them *f*	ן	אוֹתָן	3rd person

---

[3] Hebrew Alphabet

➜ Only root letter: ג ד - ז ח ט - ס ע פ צ ק ר ש

➜ Root or prefix: א - ב - ל - ש

➜ Root, prefix or suffix: ה - כ - מ - נ - ת

➜ root, prefix, suffix, infix: י - ו

---

[4] Noun Forms

Singular	Dual	Plural
A shoe	A pair of shoes	More than two shoes
נַעַל	נַעֲלַיִם	נְעָלִים
A day	Two days	More than two days
יוֹם	יוֹמַיִם	יָמִים
A week	Two weeks	More than two weeks
שָׁבוּעַ	שְׁבוּעַיִם	שָׁבוּעוֹת

---

[5] Demonstrative pronoun

		Subject	Adj.
זֶה	=	This (*m*)	This
זֹאת, זוֹ	=	This (*f*)	This
אֵלֶּה	=	These (*m/f*)	
הַהוּא	=	That (*m*)	That
הַהִיא	=	That (*f*)	That
הֵמָּה	=	Those (*m*)	Those
הֵנָּה	=	Those (*f*)	Those

Adjective always has a ה prefix

---

[6] Guttural Letters:

א - ה - ח - ע - ר

No *dagesh* – changed vowels

---

[7] Syllables

➜ Consonant with one long vowel: כָּ.

➜ Consonant with short vowel + consonant with *sheva* : נַחְ. אַרְ.

➜ Consonant with short vowel + consonant with full vowel and *dagesh hazak*: הַגָּ

Or

➜ 1, 2, or 3 preceeded by a letter with *shava* נַע.

---

[8] 7 Verb Prefix Letters

א - ת - י - נ - ה - מ - ל

---

[9] Sheva

Sheva nach (נַח)

➜ found under the letter following a short vowel.

Sheva nah (נָע)

➜ Beginning of a word.
➜ After long vowel.
➜ After a *sheva* נָח.
➜ Under a letter following a short vowel with a dagesh in the 2nd letter.
➜ Two identical letters in a row, the first letter takes a *sheva* נָע.

Chataf sheva

➜ אֱ אֲ אֳ
➜ Only under א-ה-ח-ע.
➜ The *sheva* is true to form and function, the vowel with the *sheva* is only for the fuller sound.

---

[10] Accent

Emphasis is always on last syllable of the word unless an earlier syllable is marked with a vertical line underneath the letter. For example: מֶלֶךְ

---

[11] Noun & Adjective gender number endings

masc. sing.	masc. plural
xxx	xxxים
fem. sing.	fem. plural
xxxה	xxxות

---

[12] Construct Nouns

masc. sing.	xxx
masc. plural	xxx י
fem. sing.	xxx ת
fem. plural	xxx ות

---

[13] Subject Pronouns

Singular

I *common*	• אֲנִי, אָנֹכִי	1st person
You *m,s*	אַתָּה	2nd person
You *f,s*	אַתְּ	2nd person
He *m,s*	הוּא	3rd person
She *f,s*	הִיא	3rd person

Plural

We *common*	• אָנוּ, אֲנַחְנוּ	1st person
you *m,pl*	אַתֶּם	2nd person
You *f,pl*	אַתֶּן	2nd person
They *m,pl*	• הֵם, הֵמָּה	3rd person
They *f,pl*	• הֵן, הֵנָּה	3rd person

• Either form is equally valid

---

[14] Mapik ה

➜ Direct object of verb:

שְׁמָרָה אוֹתָהּ = שְׁמָרָהּ

➜ Possessive pronoun:

דּוֹד שֶׁלָּהּ = דּוֹדָהּ

➜ Object of preposition:

יֵשׁ לָהּ = לָהּ

---

[15] Begged Keffet:

בּ - גּ - דּ - כּ - פּ - ת

Begin word + after *sheva* נָח, get dagesh.

---

[16] Vowels

Short	Long
אַ פַּתַח	אָ קָמֵץ
אֻ קֻבּוּץ	אוּ שׁוּרוּק
אִ חִירִיק חָסֵר	אִי חִירִיק מָלֵא
אָ קָמֵץ קָטָן	אוֹ, אֹ חוֹלָם
אֶ סְגוֹל	אֵ צֵירֵה

---

[17] Object of Preposition

Singular

with me *common*	עִמִּי	אִתִּי	1st person
with you *m,s*	עִמְּךָ	אִתְּךָ	2nd person
with you *f,s*	עִמָּךְ	אִתָּךְ	2nd person
with him *m,s*	עִמּוֹ	אִתּוֹ	3rd person
with her *f,s*	עִמָּהּ	אִתָּהּ	3rd person

Plural

with us *common*	עִמָּנוּ	אִתָּנוּ	1st person
with you *m,pl*	עִמָּכֶם	אַתְכֶם	2nd person
with you *f,pl*	עִמָּכֶן	אִתְּכֶן	2nd person
with them *m,pl*	עִמָּהֶם	אִתָּהֶם	3rd person
with them *f,pl*	עִמָּהֶן	אִתָּהֶן	3rd person

QUICK REFERENCE II

בס״ד

[18] Hebrew Cardinal and Ordinal Numbers

feminine		masculine		feminine		masculine
אַחַת, רִאשׁוֹנָה	1	א	אֶחָד, רִאשׁוֹן	שְׁמוֹנָה-עֶשְׂרֵה	18	י״ח	שְׁמוֹנָה-עָשָׂר
שְׁתַּיִם, שְׁנִיָּה	2	ב	שְׁנַיִם, שֵׁנִי	תִּשְׁעָה-עֶשְׂרֵה	19	י״ט	תִּשְׁעָה-עָשָׂר
שָׁלֹשׁ, שְׁלִישִׁית	3	ג	שְׁלֹשָׁה, שְׁלִישִׁי	עֶשְׂרִים	20	כ	עֶשְׂרִים
אַרְבַּע, רְבִיעִית	4	ד	אַרְבָּעָה, רְבִיעִי	עֶשְׂרִים וְאַחַת	21	כ״א	עֶשְׂרִים וְאֶחָד
חָמֵשׁ, חֲמִישִׁית	5	ה	חֲמִשָּׁה, חֲמִישִׁי	שְׁלוֹשִׁים	30	ל	שְׁלוֹשִׁים
שֵׁשׁ, שִׁשִּׁית	6	ו	שִׁשָּׁה, שִׁשִּׁי	אַרְבָּעִים	40	מ	אַרְבָּעִים
שֶׁבַע, שְׁבִיעִית	7	ז	שִׁבְעָה, שְׁבִיעִי	חֲמִשִּׁים	50	נ	חֲמִשִּׁים
שְׁמוֹנֶה, שְׁמִינִית	8	ח	שְׁמוֹנָה, שְׁמִינִי	שִׁשִּׁים	60	ס	שִׁשִּׁים
תֵּשַׁע, תְּשִׁיעִית	9	ט	תִּשְׁעָה, תְּשִׁיעִי	שִׁבְעִים	70	ע	שִׁבְעִים
עֶשֶׂר, עֲשִׂירִית	10	י	עֲשָׂרָה, עֲשִׂירִי	שְׁמוֹנִים	80	פ	שְׁמוֹנִים

After ten, the ordinal number is formed by adding the definite article, e.g. הָאֶחָד עָשָׂר, הַשְּׁלֹשִׁים in multiples of ten, hundreds etc. There is no Distinction between masculine and feminine.

					90	צ	תִּשְׁעִים
					100	ק	מֵאָה
					200	ר	מָאתַיִם
					300	ש	שְׁלֹשׁ מֵאוֹת
					1000	א	אֶלֶף
					2000	ב	אַלְפַּיִם
					3000	ג	שְׁלוֹשֶׁת אֲלָפִים

feminine		masculine			
אַחַת-עֶשְׂרֵה	11	י״א	אַחַד-עָשָׂר
שְׁתֵּים-עֶשְׂרֵה	12	י״ב	שְׁנֵים-עָשָׂר
שָׁלֹשׁ-עֶשְׂרֵה	13	י״ג	שְׁלוֹשָׁה-עָשָׂר
אַרְבַּע-עֶשְׂרֵה	14	י״ד	אַרְבָּעָה-עָשָׂר
חֲמֵשׁ-עֶשְׂרֵה	15	ט״ו	חֲמִשָּׁה-עָשָׂר
שֵׁשׁ-עֶשְׂרֵה	16	ט״ז	שִׁשָּׁה-עָשָׂר
שְׁבַע-עֶשְׂרֵה	17	י״ז	שִׁבְעָה-עָשָׂר

חֲמֵשֶׁת אֲלָפִים		חֲמֵשֶׁת אֲלָפִים
מָאתַיִם שְׁלוֹשִׁים	5235	מָאתַיִם שְׁלוֹשִׁים
וְחָמֵשׁ		וַחֲמִשָּׁה

[21] Dropping Letter Chart

פ	ע	ל
א	ו	ה
נ	י	נ
		ל

[22] Suffix Letters

The letters for the direct object of verb, the possessive pronoun, and the object of a preposition, when attached directly to the verb, noun or preposition are:

Me, mine (m, f)	אִי, נִי
Your (m)	ךָ
Yours (f)	אָךְ
Him, his	אָיו, הוּ, ו, נוּ
Her, hers	אָהּ, נָהּ
Us, our	נוּ
Yours (m, pl)	כֶם
Yours (f, pl)	כֶן
Them, theirs (m,pl)	ם or הֶם
Them, theirs (f, pl)	ן or הֶן

[23] Possessive Pronoun Endings

Aunts	Aunt	Uncles	Uncle	
דּוֹדוֹת	דּוֹדָה	דּוֹדִים	דּוֹד	
				Singular
דּוֹדוֹתַי	דּוֹדָתִי	דּוֹדַי	דּוֹדִי	שֶׁלִּי My
דּוֹדוֹתֶיךָ	דּוֹדָתְךָ	דּוֹדֶיךָ	דּוֹדְךָ	שֶׁלְּךָ Your m
דּוֹדוֹתַיִךְ	דּוֹדָתֵךְ	דּוֹדַיִךְ	דּוֹדֵךְ	שֶׁלָּךְ Your f
דּוֹדוֹתָיו	דּוֹדָתוֹ	דּוֹדָיו	דּוֹדוֹ	שֶׁלּוֹ His
דּוֹדוֹתֶיהָ	דּוֹדָתָהּ	דּוֹדֶיהָ	דּוֹדָהּ	שֶׁלָּהּ Her, hers
				Plural
דּוֹדוֹתֵינוּ	דּוֹדָתֵנוּ	דּוֹדֵינוּ	דּוֹדֵנוּ	שֶׁלָּנוּ Our
דּוֹדוֹתֵיכֶם	דּוֹדַתְכֶם	דּוֹדֵיכֶם	דּוֹדְכֶם	שֶׁלָּכֶם Your m
דּוֹדוֹתֵיכֶן	דּוֹדַתְכֶן	דּוֹדֵיכֶן	דּוֹדְכֶן	שֶׁלָּכֶן Your f
דּוֹדוֹתֵיהֶם	דּוֹדָתָם	דּוֹדֵיהֶם	דּוֹדָם	שֶׁלָּהֶם Their m
דּוֹדוֹתֵיהֶן	דּוֹדָתָן	דּוֹדֵיהֶן	דּוֹדָן	שֶׁלָּהֶן Their f

[19] Number Person Gender Tense

number	person	gender	past	present	future
S I N G U L A R	1	M	xxxxתִּי	XXX, xXֹוX	XXXX א
	1	F	xxxxתִּי	XXXֶֶת, הXXXX	XXXX א
	2	M	xxxתָּ	XXX, xXֹוX	XXXX ת
	2	F	xxxתְּ	XXXֶֶת, הXXXX	XXXXי ת
	3	M	xxx	XXX, xXֹוX	XXX י
	3	F	xxxָה	XXXֶֶת, הXXXX	XXXX ת
P L U R A L	1	M	xxxxנוּ	XXXִים	XXX נ
	1	F	xxxxנוּ	XXXוֹת	XXX נ
	2	M	xxxxתֶּם	XXXִים	XXXוּ ת
	2	F	xxxxתֶּן	XXXוֹת	XXXXנָה ת
	3	M	xxxxוּ	XXXִים	XXXוּ י
	3	F	xxxxוּ	XXXוֹת	XXXXנָה ת

[24] Binyanim

		CAUSATIVE	INTENSIVE	SIMPLE		
		מַפְעִיל	מְפַעֵל	פּוֹעֵל	Present	A C T I V E
	REFLEXIVE					
Present	מִתְפַּעֵל	הִפְעִיל	פִּעֵל	פָּעַל	Past	
Past	הִתְפַּעֵל	יַפְעִיל	יְפַעֵל	יִפְעַ'ל or יִפְעֹל	Future	
Future	יִתְפַּעֵל	מֻפְעָל	מְפֻעָל	נִפְעָל	Present	P A S S I V E
		הֻפְעַל	פֻּעַל	נִפְעַל	Past	
		יֻפְעַל	יְפֻעַל	יִפָּעֵל	Future	

[20] Prefix Letters

Prefix	Past	Present	Future	Noun/Adj	Poss. end Direct Object	Special Notes
א			I will Hispa'el			
את			I will			
ב				In, with, at on, among, within, into, by, of as when		
ה	hiph'il hooph'al	Definite noun		The definitive or interrogative		
חת				hispa'el		
ו	Reversing ו (and)	And	Reversing ו (and)	And	ו Changes past to future, and future to past in תג״ך	
י			He will			
יxxxו			They will (m,pl)			
ית			Hispa'el He will			
יתxxxו			Hispa'el They will			
כ				Like, as, Similarly		
כש				כש + noun/adj = when		
ל				To, for		w/verb makor forms infinitive
מ		pi'el, hiph'il, hispa'el, poo'al, hooph'al		From, of more than, since		Sign of a noun
מת		hispa'el				Sign of a noun
נ	niph'al	niph'al	We will			
נת			hispa'el we will			
ש				That, which, who, whom, because, since for		
ת			You (m,s) She (f,s)			
תxxxי			You will (f,s)			
תxx			You will (m,s) She will (f,s)			
תxxxxי			You will (f,s)			
תxxxxnה			You/they will (f,pl)			
תxxxו hispa'el			You will (m,pl)			
תxxxxnה Hispa'el			You/they will (f,pl)			

Suffix/Infix Letters

	Suffix / infix	Past	Present	Future	Noun/Adj	Poss. end Direct Object	Special Notes
[25] s u f f i x	אָה	She was	She is		Replaces ל prefix noun/adj.(f,s)	Hers, her	Her = obj. of prep.
	ו	They (m & f, pl)		They, you (m,pl), command		His (ו), him (ו)	Her = obj. of prep.
	וֹת		(f,pl)			(f,pl)	
	חוּ					His or him	
	חוֹן					Their, them (f,pl)	
	אי					Me,my,mine (m & f, s)	
	אִי					Me, my mine (m,pl)	
	אֵי			Construct noun (m,pl)			
	תִּי	First person (m & f, s)					
	י			Command form (f,s)			
	xxxִים		(m,pl)	(m,pl)			
	ךְ (final כ)					You (m & f,s)	Obj or prep
	כֶם					You (m,pl)	Obj or prep
	כֶן					You (f,pl)	Obj or prep
	ם					You, them theirs (m,pl)	Obj or prep
	הֶם					You, them theirs (m,pl)	Obj or prep
	נה			You/they will (f,pl)		Her = direct object	
	ת	You (m & f, s)					
	תֶּם	You (m,pl)					
	נוּ	We (m & f, pl)				We, our, ours (m & f, pl)	
	תֶּן	You (f,pl)					
	אֵת				Construct noun (f,s)		
	אָאת		(f,s)		(f,s)		
[26] i n f i x	xxֹוx				(m,f. s,pl)	Noun, adj. Adjective	
	xֹxx					Noun, adj.	
	xֹxx					Noun, adj.	
	xxֹxx	Hiph'il (3 pers)	Hiph'il w/present tense	Hiph'il w/future tense prefix		Infinitive, absolute, noun/adj.	
	xxx					Noun, adj.	
	xxxה					Gerund	Gerund is noun form of verb ending in 'ing'
	xxxה						

QUICK REFERENCE III

Complete Root / 7 Binyanim

28 — Past Tense | 27 — Root קצר

3rd	2nd (f)	2nd (m)	1st	3rd (f)	3rd (m)	2nd (f)	2nd (m)	1st	מ	ל	כ	ב	Relative/Absolute	Category
קָצְרוּ	קְצַרְתֶּן	קְצַרְתֶּם	קָצַרְנוּ	קָצְרָה	קָצַר	קָצַרְתְּ	קָצַרְתָּ	קָצַרְתִּי	מִקְצָר	לִקְצֹר	כְּקָצַר	בְּקָצַר	קָצוֹר, קָצַר	פָּעַל
קָצְרוּ	קְצַרְתֶּן	קְצַרְתֶּם	קָצַרְנוּ	קָצְרָה	קָצַר	קָצַרְתְּ	קָצַרְתָּ	קָצַרְתִּי	מִקְצָר	לִקְצַר	כְּקָצַר	בְּקָצַר	קָצַר	פָּעַל
הִקְצִירוּ	הִקְצַרְתֶּן	הִקְצַרְתֶּם	הִקְצַרְנוּ	הִקְצִירָה	הִקְצִיר	הִקְצַרְתְּ	הִקְצַרְתָּ	הִקְצַרְתִּי	מַהְקְצִיר	לְהַקְצִיר	כְּהַקְצִיר	בְּהַקְצִיר	הַקְצֵר, מַקְצִיר	הִפְעִיל
הִתְקַצְּרוּ	הִתְקַצַּרְתֶּן	הִתְקַצַּרְתֶּם	הִתְקַצַּרְנוּ	הִתְקַצְּרָה	הִתְקַצֵּר	הִתְקַצַּרְתְּ	הִתְקַצַּרְתָּ	הִתְקַצַּרְתִּי	מִהְתְקַצֵּר	לְהִתְקַצֵּר	כְּהִתְקַצֵּר	בְּהִתְקַצֵּר	הִתְקַצֵּר	הִתְפָּעֵל
נִקְצְרוּ	נִקְצַרְתֶּן	נִקְצַרְתֶּם	נִקְצַרְנוּ	נִקְצְרָה	נִקְצַר	נִקְצַרְתְּ	נִקְצַרְתָּ	נִקְצַרְתִּי	מִקְצָר	לְהִקָּצֵר	כְּהִקָּצֵר	בְּהִקָּצֵר	נִקְצוֹר, הִקָּצֵר	נִפְעַל
קָצְרוּ	קְצַרְתֶּן	קְצַרְתֶּם	קָצַרְנוּ	קָצְרָה	קָצַר	קָצַרְתְּ	קָצַרְתָּ	קָצַרְתִּי	None	None	None	None	קָצוֹר	פָּעַל
הֻקְצְרוּ	הֻקְצַרְתֶּן	הֻקְצַרְתֶּם	הֻקְצַרְנוּ	הֻקְצְרָה	הֻקְצַר	הֻקְצַרְתְּ	הֻקְצַרְתָּ	הֻקְצַרְתִּי	None	None	None	None	הֻקְצַר	הֻפְעַל

31 — Command (imperative)

Category	Plural F	Plural M	Singular F	Singular M
פָּעַל	קְצֹרְנָה	קִצְרוּ	קִצְרִי	קְצֹר
פָּעַל	קְצַרְנָה	קִצְרוּ	קִצְרִי	קְצַר
הִפְעִיל	הַקְצֵרְנָה	הַקְצִירוּ	הַקְצִירִי	הַקְצֵר
הִתְפָּעֵל	הִתְקַצֵּרְנָה	הִתְקַצְּרוּ	הִתְקַצְּרִי	הִתְקַצֵּר
נִפְעַל	הִקָּצֵרְנָה	הִקָּצְרוּ	הִקָּצְרִי	הִקָּצֵר
פָּעַל	None	None	None	None
הֻפְעַל	None	None	None	None

30 — Future Tense

3rd (f)	3rd (m)	2nd (f)	2nd (m)	1st	3rd (f)	3rd (m)	2nd (f)	2nd (m)	1st
תִּקְצֹרְנָה	יִקְצְרוּ	תִּקְצֹרְנָה	תִּקְצְרוּ	נִקְצֹר	תִּקְצֹר	יִקְצֹר	תִּקְצְרִי	תִּקְצֹר	אֶקְצֹר
תִּקְצַרְנָה	יִקְצְרוּ	תִּקְצַרְנָה	תִּקְצְרוּ	נִקְצַר	תִּקְצַר	יִקְצַר	תִּקְצְרִי	תִּקְצַר	אֶקְצַר
תַּקְצֵרְנָה	יַקְצִירוּ	תַּקְצֵרְנָה	תַּקְצִירוּ	נַקְצִיר	תַּקְצִיר	יַקְצִיר	תַּקְצִירִי	תַּקְצִיר	אַקְצִיר
תִּתְקַצֵּרְנָה	יִתְקַצְּרוּ	תִּתְקַצֵּרְנָה	תִּתְקַצְּרוּ	נִתְקַצֵּר	תִּתְקַצֵּר	יִתְקַצֵּר	תִּתְקַצְּרִי	תִּתְקַצֵּר	אֶתְקַצֵּר
תִּקָּצַרְנָה	יִקָּצְרוּ	תִּקָּצַרְנָה	תִּקָּצְרוּ	נִקָּצֵר	תִּקָּצֵר	יִקָּצֵר	תִּקָּצְרִי	תִּקָּצֵר	אֶקָּצֵר
תִּקְצֹרְנָה	יִקְצְרוּ	תִּקְצֹרְנָה	תִּקְצְרוּ	נִקְצֹר	תִּקְצֹר	יִקְצֹר	תִּקְצְרִי	תִּקְצֹר	אֶקְצֹר
תֻּקְצַרְנָה	יֻקְצְרוּ	תֻּקְצַרְנָה	תֻּקְצְרוּ	נֻקְצַר	תֻּקְצַר	יֻקְצַר	תֻּקְצְרִי	תֻּקְצַר	אֻקְצַר

29 — Present Tense

Category	Plural F	Plural M	Singular F	Singular M
פָּעַל	קוֹצְרוֹת	קוֹצְרִים	קוֹצֶרֶת (קוֹצְרָה)	קוֹצֵר
פָּעַל	מִקְצָרוֹת	מִקְצָרִים	מִקְצֶרֶת	מִקְצָר
הִפְעִיל	מַקְצִירוֹת	מַקְצִירִים	מַקְצִירָה (מַקְצִירָה)	מַקְצִיר
הִתְפָּעֵל	מִתְקַצְּרוֹת	מִתְקַצְּרִים	מִתְקַצֶּרֶת (מִתְקַצְּרָה)	מִתְקַצֵּר
נִפְעַל	נִקְצָרוֹת	נִקְצָרִים	נִקְצֶרֶת (נִקְצְרָה)	נִקְצָר
פָּעַל	מִקְצָרוֹת	מִקְצָרִים	מִקְצֶרֶת	מִקְצָר
הֻפְעַל	מֻקְצָרוֹת	מֻקְצָרִים	מֻקְצֶרֶת	מֻקְצָר

Dropping Letters Simple Binyan, Intensive Binyan & Causative Binyan

33 — Past Tense | 32 — Dropping Letter Forms

3rd	2nd (f)	2nd (m)	1st	3rd (f)	3rd (m)	2nd (f)	2nd (m)	1st	מ	ל	כ	ב	Relative/Absolute	Root	Category
אָכְלוּ	אֲכַלְתֶּן	אֲכַלְתֶּם	אָכַלְנוּ	אָכְלָה	אָכַל	אָכַלְתְּ	אָכַלְתָּ	אָכַלְתִּי	מַאֲכָל	לֶאֱכֹל	כֶּאֱכֹל	בֶּאֱכֹל	אָכוֹל, אֱכֹל	אכל	פָּעַל פ״א
יָשְׁבוּ	יְשַׁבְתֶּן	יְשַׁבְתֶּם	יָשַׁבְנוּ	יָשְׁבָה	יָשַׁב	יָשַׁבְתְּ	יָשַׁבְתָּ	יָשַׁבְתִּי	מֹשֶׁבֶת	לָשֶׁבֶת	כְּשֶׁבֶת	בְּשֶׁבֶת	יָשׁוֹב, שֶׁבֶת	ישב	פָּעַל פ״י
נָפְלוּ	נְפַלְתֶּן	נְפַלְתֶּם	נָפַלְנוּ	נָפְלָה	נָפַל	נָפַלְתְּ	נָפַלְתָּ	נָפַלְתִּי	מִנְפָּל	לִנְפֹּל	כִּנְפֹּל	בִּנְפֹּל	נָפוֹל, נָפֹל	נפל	פָּעַל פ״נ
קָמוּ	קַמְתֶּן	קַמְתֶּם	קַמְנוּ	קָמָה	קָם	קַמְתְּ	קַמְתָּ	קַמְתִּי	מַקוֹם	לָקוּם	כְּקוּם	בְּקוּם	קוֹם, קוּם	קום	פָּעַל ע״ו
רָאוּ	רְאִיתֶן	רְאִיתֶם	רָאִינוּ	רָאֲתָה	רָאָה	רָאִית	רָאִיתָ	רָאִיתִי	מַרְאוֹת	לִרְאוֹת	כִּרְאוֹת	בִּרְאוֹת	רָאֹה, רָאֹה	ראה	פָּעַל ל״ה
קָרְאוּ	קְרָאתֶן	קְרָאתֶם	קָרָאנוּ	קָרְאָה	קָרָא	קָרָאת	קָרָאתָ	קָרָאתִי	מִקְרָא	לִקְרֹא	כִּקְרֹא	בִּקְרֹא	קָרוֹא, קְרֹא	קרא	פָּעַל ל״א
צִוּוּ	צִוִּיתֶן	צִוִּיתֶם	צִוִּינוּ	צִוְּתָה	צִוָּה	צִוִּית	צִוִּיתָ	צִוִּיתִי	מְצַוֹּת	לְצַוֹּת	כְּצַוֹּת		צַוֹּת	צוה	פָּעַל ל״ה,ע״י
הֶאֱכִילוּ	הֶאֱכַלְתֶּן	הֶאֱכַלְתֶּם	הֶאֱכַלְנוּ	הֶאֱכִילָה	הֶאֱכִיל	הֶאֱכַלְתְּ	הֶאֱכַלְתָּ	הֶאֱכַלְתִּי	מַהֲאֲכִיל	לְהַאֲכִיל	כְּהַאֲכִיל	בְּהַאֲכִיל	הַאֲכֵל, מַאֲכִיל	אכל	הִפְעִיל פ״א
הוֹרִידוּ	הוֹרַדְתֶּן	הוֹרַדְתֶּם	הוֹרַדְנוּ	הוֹרִידָה	הוֹרִיד	הוֹרַדְתְּ	הוֹרַדְתָּ	הוֹרַדְתִּי	מְהוֹרִיד	לְהוֹרִיד	כְּהוֹרִיד	בְּהוֹרִיד	הוֹרֵד, הוֹרִיד	ירד	הִפְעִיל פ״י
הִפִּילוּ	הִפַּלְתֶּן	הִפַּלְתֶּם	הִפַּלְנוּ	הִפִּילָה	הִפִּיל	הִפַּלְתְּ	הִפַּלְתָּ	הִפַּלְתִּי	מַהְפִּיל	לְהַפִּיל	כְּהַפִּיל	בְּהַפִּיל	הַפֵּל, הַפִּיל	נפל	הִפְעִיל פ״נ
הֵקִימוּ	הֲקִימוֹתֶן	הֲקִימוֹתֶם	הֲקִימוֹנוּ	הֵקִימָה	הֵקִים	הֲקִימוֹת	הֲקִימוֹתָ	הֲקִימוֹתִי	מְהָקִים	לְהָקִים	כְּהָקִים	בְּהָקִים	הָקֵם, הָקִים	קום	הִפְעִיל ע״ו-י׳
הֶרְאוּ	הֶרְאֵיתֶן	הֶרְאֵיתֶם	הֶרְאֵינוּ	הֶרְאֲתָה	הֶרְאָה	הֶרְאֵית	הֶרְאֵיתָ	הֶרְאֵיתִי	מַהְרְאוֹת	לְהַרְאוֹת	כְּהַרְאוֹת	בְּהַרְאוֹת	הַרְאֵה, הַרְאֹה	ראה	הִפְעִיל ל״ה

36 — Command (imperative)

Category	Plural F	Plural M	Singular F	Singular M
פָּעַל פ״א	אֱכֹלְנָה	אִכְלוּ	אִכְלִי	אֱכֹל
פָּעַל פ״י	שֵׁבְנָה	שְׁבוּ	שְׁבִי	שֵׁב
פָּעַל פ״נ	נְפֹלְנָה	נִפְלוּ	נִפְלִי	נְפֹל
פָּעַל ע״ו	קֹמְנָה	קוּמוּ	קוּמִי	קוּם
פָּעַל ל״ה	רְאֶינָה	רְאוּ	רְאִי	רְאֵה
פָּעַל ל״א	קְרֶאנָה	קִרְאוּ	קִרְאִי	קְרָא
פָּעַל ל״ה	צַוֶּינָה	צַוּוּ	צַוִּי	צַוֵּה
הִפְעִיל פ״א	הַאֲכֵלְנָה	הַאֲכִילוּ	הַאֲכִילִי	הַאֲכֵל
הִפְעִיל פ״י	הוֹרֵדְנָה	הוֹרִידוּ	הוֹרִידִי	הוֹרֵד
הִפְעִיל פ״נ	הַפֵּלְנָה	הַפִּילוּ	הַפִּילִי	הַפֵּל
הִפְעִיל ע״ו	הָקֵמְנָה	הָקִימוּ	הָקִימִי	הָקֵם
הִפְעִיל ל״ה	הַרְאֶינָה	הַרְאוּ	הַרְאִי	הַרְאֵה

35 — Future Tense

3rd (f)	3rd (m)	2nd (f)	2nd (m)	1st	3rd (f)	3rd (m)	2nd (f)	2nd (m)	1st
תֹּאכַלְנָה	יֹאכְלוּ	תֹּאכַלְנָה	תֹּאכְלוּ	נֹאכַל	תֹּאכַל	יֹאכַל	תֹּאכְלִי	תֹּאכַל	אֹכַל
תֵּשַׁבְנָה	יֵשְׁבוּ	תֵּשַׁבְנָה	תֵּשְׁבוּ	נֵשֵׁב	תֵּשֵׁב	יֵשֵׁב	תֵּשְׁבִי	תֵּשֵׁב	אֵשֵׁב
תִּפֹּלְנָה	יִפְּלוּ	תִּפֹּלְנָה	תִּפְּלוּ	נִפֹּל	תִּפֹּל	יִפֹּל	תִּפְּלִי	תִּפֹּל	אֶפֹּל
תְּקֹמְנָה	יָקוּמוּ	תְּקֹמְנָה	תָּקוּמוּ	נָקוּם	תָּקוּם	יָקוּם	תָּקוּמִי	תָּקוּם	אָקוּם
תִּרְאֶינָה	יִרְאוּ	תִּרְאֶינָה	תִּרְאוּ	נִרְאֶה	תִּרְאֶה	יִרְאֶה	תִּרְאִי	תִּרְאֶה	אֶרְאֶה
תִּקְרֶאנָה	יִקְרְאוּ	תִּקְרֶאנָה	תִּקְרְאוּ	נִקְרָא	תִּקְרָא	יִקְרָא	תִּקְרְאִי	תִּקְרָא	אֶקְרָא
תְּצַוֶּינָה	יְצַוּוּ	תְּצַוֶּינָה	תְּצַוּוּ	נְצַוֶּה	תְּצַוֶּה	יְצַוֶּה	תְּצַוִּי	תְּצַוֶּה	אֲצַוֶּה
תַּאֲכֵלְנָה	יַאֲכִילוּ	תַּאֲכֵלְנָה	תַּאֲכִילוּ	נַאֲכִיל	תַּאֲכִיל	יַאֲכִיל	תַּאֲכִילִי	תַּאֲכִיל	אַאֲכִיל
תּוֹרֵדְנָה	יוֹרִידוּ	תּוֹרֵדְנָה	תּוֹרִידוּ	נוֹרִיד	תּוֹרִיד	יוֹרִיד	תּוֹרִידִי	תּוֹרִיד	אוֹרִיד
תַּפֵּלְנָה	יַפִּילוּ	תַּפֵּלְנָה	תַּפִּילוּ	נַפִּיל	תַּפִּיל	יַפִּיל	תַּפִּילִי	תַּפִּיל	אַפִּיל
תְּקֵמְנָה	יָקִימוּ	תְּקֵמְנָה	תָּקִימוּ	נָקִים	תָּקִים	יָקִים	תָּקִימִי	תָּקִים	אָקִים
תַּרְאֶינָה	יַרְאוּ	תַּרְאֶינָה	תַּרְאוּ	נַרְאֶה	תַּרְאֶה	יַרְאֶה	תַּרְאִי	תַּרְאֶה	אַרְאֶה

34 — Present Tense

Category	Plural F	Plural M	Singular F	Singular M
פָּעַל פ״א	אוֹכְלוֹת	אוֹכְלִים	אוֹכֶלֶת (אוֹכְלָה)	אוֹכֵל
פָּעַל פ״י	יוֹשְׁבוֹת	יוֹשְׁבִים	יוֹשֶׁבֶת (יוֹשְׁבָה)	יוֹשֵׁב
פָּעַל פ״נ	נוֹפְלוֹת	נוֹפְלִים	נוֹפֶלֶת (נוֹפְלָה)	נוֹפֵל
פָּעַל ע״ו	קָמוֹת	קָמִים	קָמָה	קָם
פָּעַל ל״ה	רוֹאוֹת	רוֹאִים	רוֹאָה	רוֹאֶה
פָּעַל ל״א	קוֹרְאוֹת	קוֹרְאִים	קוֹרֵאת (קוֹרְאָה)	קוֹרֵא
פָּעַל ל״ה	מְצַוּוֹת	מְצַוִּים	מְצַוָּה	מְצַוֶּה
הִפְעִיל פ״א	מַאֲכִילוֹת	מַאֲכִילִים	מַאֲכֶלֶת (מַאֲכִילָה)	מַאֲכִיל
הִפְעִיל פ״י	מוֹרִידוֹת	מוֹרִידִים	מוֹרֶדֶת (מוֹרִידָה)	מוֹרִיד
הִפְעִיל פ״נ	מַפִּילוֹת	מַפִּילִים	מַפֶּלֶת (מַפִּילָה)	מַפִּיל
הִפְעִיל ע״ו	מְקִימוֹת	מְקִימִים	מְקִימָה	מֵקִים
הִפְעִיל ל״ה	מַרְאוֹת	מַרְאִים	מַרְאָה	מַרְאֶה

בס"ד

ARAMAIC VERB AND NOUN CHART

VERB FORMS `38`

Passive אתפעל	Causative אפעל	Intensive פעל	Simple פעל	See notes on bottom of page
איתפעל	אפעל	פעל	פעל	Past עבר
נתפעל	נפעל	נפעל	ניפע(ו)ל	Future עתיד
מי(ת)פעל	מפעל	מפעל	פע(י)ל	Present הווה
לאי(ת)פעולי	לאפעולי	(ל)פעולי	(ל)מיפעל	Infinitive שם פועל

NOUN FORMS `37`

Feminine		Masculine		See notes on bottom of page
Plural	Sing.	Plural	Sing	
אן	אא/אה	אין/אי		A book — General נפרד
את	את	אי	XXX	The book of Shmos — Construct נסמך
אתא	אתא אתי/אא	יא	אא	The book — Specific ידוע

Verb tenses, gender and person

Present `41`		Future `40`		Past `39`		See notes on bottom of page	
Plural	Singular	Plural	Singular	Plural	Singular		
		נX	אX	נא/נן/(ך)	אית/אי/את	Masculine	1st person
		נX	אX	נא/נן/(ך)	אית/אי/את	Feminine	
		תאון/תאתון/תא	תX	אתון/אתו	את	Masculine	2nd person
		תאן/תאתון/תאך	תאין/א(י)	אתון/(אתן)	את	Feminine	
אין		נאו/לאו/לאי/ליאון	יX/לX/נX	או/XXX/א	-----	Masculine	3rd person
אן	אX/אה	ת/לאן	תX	אן/אX	את/אה/אX	Feminine	

PRONOUNS `44`

I .... אנא
You .... את / אנת
He .... ניהו / איהו
She .... ניהי / איהי
We .... אנחנא / אנן
You .... אתו / אתון
They (m) .... אינהו / נינהו / אינון
They (f) .... אינהי / נינהי

POSSESIVE PRONOUNS `43`
(Also Direct Objects & Objects of Preposition)

My .... דידי
Your .... דידך
His .... דידיה
Her .... דידה
Our .... דידנא / דידן
Your (pl) .... דידכון / דידכו
Their (m) .... דידהון / דידהו
Their (f) .... דידהי

DEMONSTRATIVES `42`

This (m) .... האי / דין
This (f) .... הא / דא
These .... הני / אילן
That (m) .... האיך / ההוא
That (f) .... הך / ההיא
Those .... הנהו / הנך / הני
This/ That .... אידי / ואידי
This (comp.) .... אידך
That (comp.) .... אינך

NUMBERS `47`

1 .... חדא / חד
2 .... תרתי / תרי / תרין
3 .... תלת / תלתא
6 .... שית / שתא
8 .... תמני / תמניא
10 .... עסר / עסרא
½ .... פלגא
⅓ .... תתא
¼ .... רבעה
⅙ .... שחית

ARAMAIC   HEBREW `46`

ת	ש
ר	נ
ד	ז
ע	צ
ט	צ

Notes for above charts: `45`

- X, x = the 3 letter root of a word, or (in one example) each of the root letters.
- **LARGE** letters indicate the identifying signs for tense and level of activity.
- ( ) = letters which are found less frequently as identifying signs for tense and level of activity.

© Rabbi Shalom Gold
Pirchei Shoshanim 2003
732-370-3344 / www.dikduk@shemayisrael.com

Background pictures:
Pg. 1: Hebron cave of patriarchs
Pg. 2-3: Western Wall
Pg. 4: grave of Rachel

	CAUSATIVE	INTENSIVE	SIMPLE
A C T I V E — Present	מַקְטִיל	מְקַטֵּל	קוֹטֵל
Past	הִקְטִיל	קִטֵּל	קָטַל
Future	יַקְטִיל	יְקַטֵּל	יִקְטֹל or יִקְטוֹל
P A S S I V E — Present	מֻקְטָל	מְקֻטָּל	נִקְטָל
Past	הֻקְטַל	קֻטַּל	נִקְטַל
Future	יֻקְטַל	יְקֻטַּל	יִקָּטֵל

REFLEXIVE

Present	מִתְקַטֵּל
Past	הִתְקַטֵּל
Future	יִתְקַטֵּל

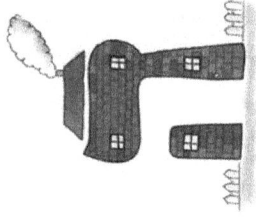

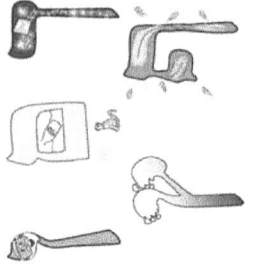

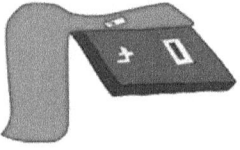

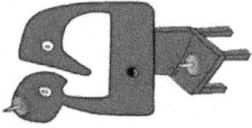

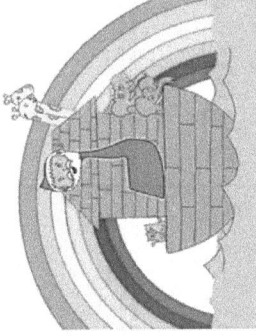

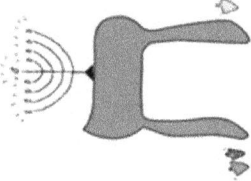

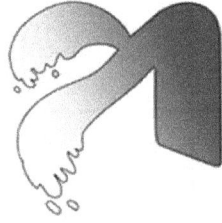

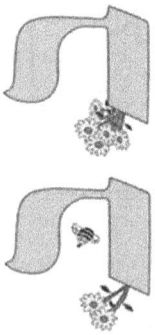

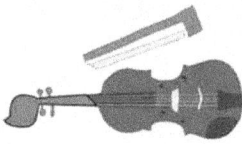

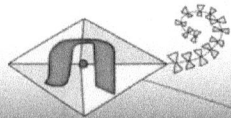

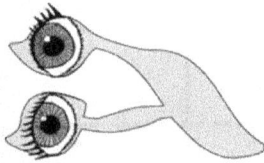

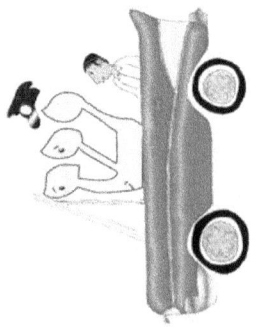

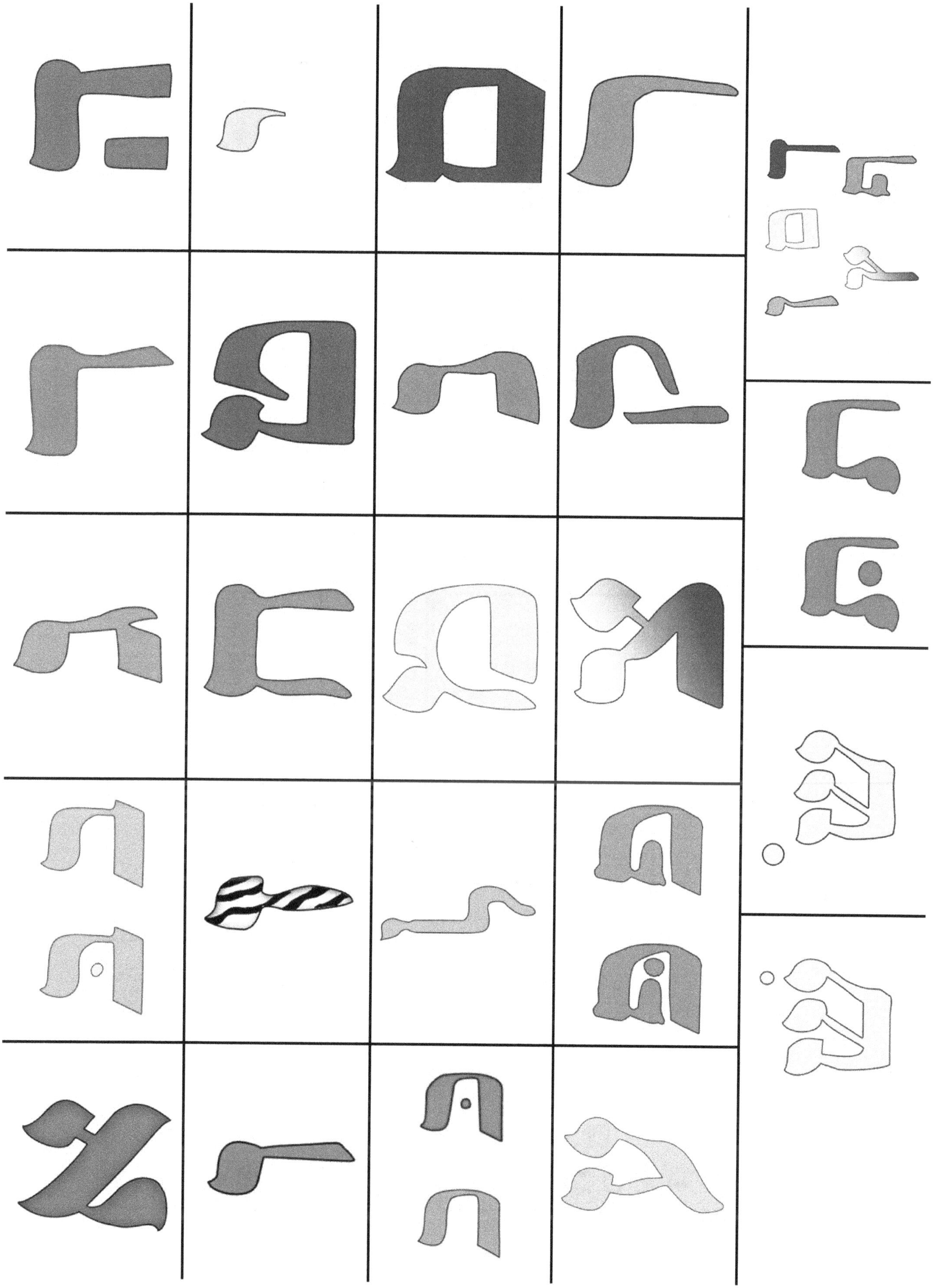

NUMBER	PERSON	GENDER	PAST	PRESENT	FUTURE
SINGULAR	1	M	I			
	1	F	I			
	2	M	You			
	2	F	You			
	3	M	He			
	3	F	She			
PLURAL	1	M	We			
	1	F	We			
	2	M	You			
	2	F	You			
	3	M	They			
	3	F	They			

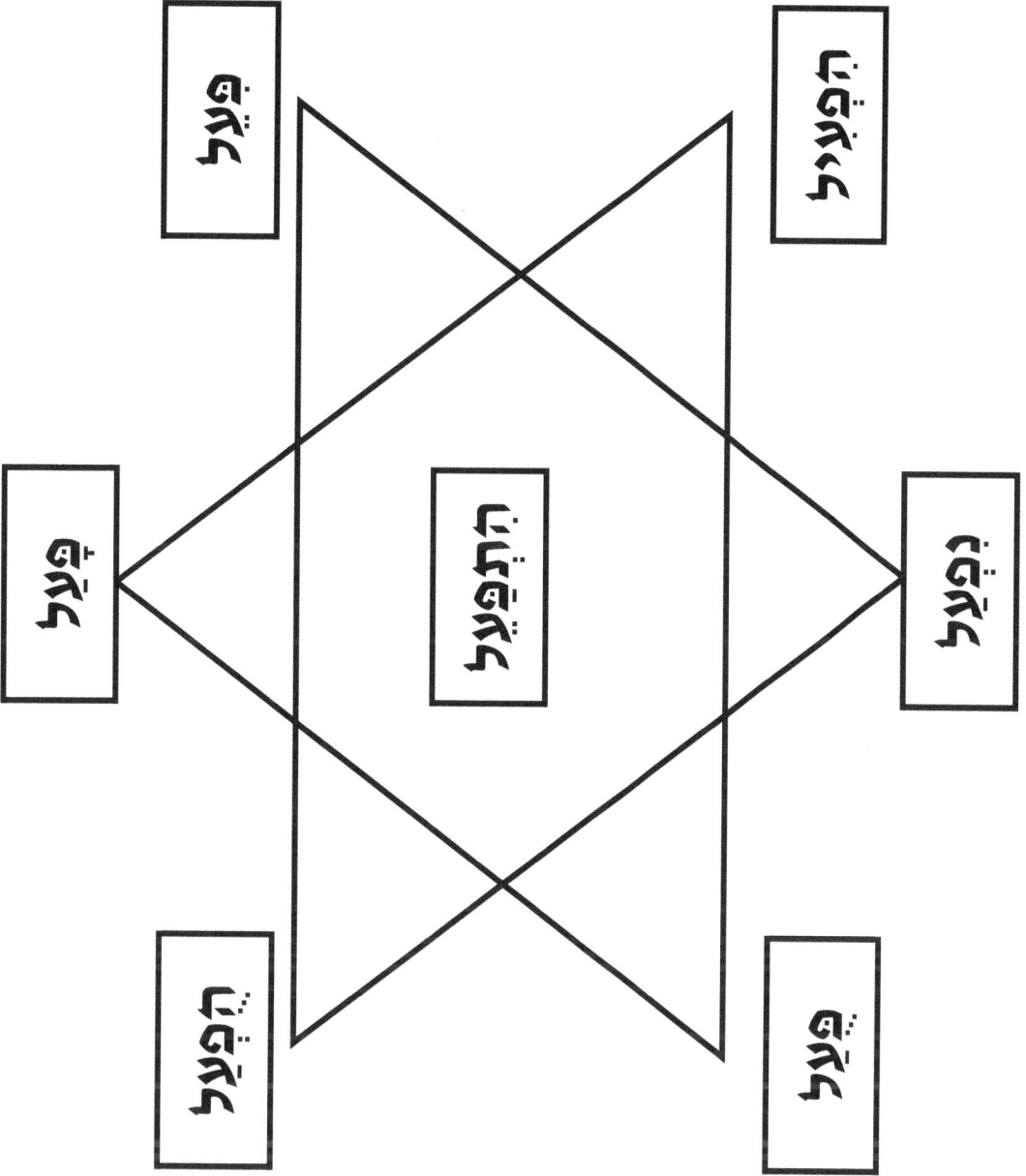

	SIMPLE	INTENSIVE	CAUSATIVE	REFLEXIVE
ACTIVE Present	קֹטֵל	מְקַטֵּל	מַקְטִיל	מִתְקַטֵּל
ACTIVE Past	קָטַל	קִטֵּל	הִקְטִיל	הִתְקַטֵּל
ACTIVE Future	יִקְטֹל or יִקְטַל	יְקַטֵּל	יַקְטִיל	יִתְקַטֵּל
PASSIVE Present	נִקְטָל	מְקֻטָּל	מֻקְטָל	
PASSIVE Past	נִקְטַל	קֻטַּל	הֻקְטַל	
PASSIVE Future	יִקָּטֵל	יְקֻטַּל	יֻקְטַל	

NUMBER	PERSON	GENDER	PAST	PRESENT	FUTURE
SINGULAR	1	M			
	1	F			
	2	M	You	You	You
	2	F	You	You	You
	3	M	He	He	He
	3	F	She	She	She
PLURAL	1	M	We	We	We
	1	F	We	We	We
	2	M	You	You	You
	2	F	You	You	You
	3	M	They	They	They
	3	F	They	They	They

VERB BINYAN DITTY

פָּעַל – פִּעֵל – הִפְעִיל – הִתְפַּעֵל – פֻּעַל – הֻפְעַל

- ❖ The פָּעַל *binyan* has a *kametz* under the first root letter. The פִּעֵל *binyan* has a short vowel, either a *patach* or a *chirik,* under the first root letter, and a full vowel under the second root letter with a *dagesh chazak* in it. The הִפְעִיל *binyan* has a ה prefix with a *chirik* under the ה. And the הִתְפַּעֵל has a הת prefix with a *chirik* under the ה and a *sheva nach* under the ת.

- ❖ In the passive forms the נִפְעַל *binyan* must have a נ prefix with a *chirik*. And the פֻּעַל *binyan* has a *kubutz* under the first root letter, a full vowel under the second root letter with a *dagesh chazak* in it. Finally in the past tense, the הֻפְעַל *binyan* must have a ה prefix with a *kubutz,* and a *sheva nach* under the first root letter.

- ❖ Five of the *binyanim* must have a מ prefix in the present tense; they are the Intensive Active and Passive, the Casuative Active and Passive, and the Reflexive.

- ❖ The Intensive Present tense must have a מ prefix with a *sheva na,* followed by a root letter with a short vowel.

- ❖ If the short vowel is a *patach* or a *chirik,* it indicates the Intensive Active Present tense – מְפַעֵל-

- ❖ If the short vowel under the first root letter is a *kubutz,* it indicates the Intensive Passive Present tense – מְפֻעַל -

- ❖ If the מ prefix has a *patach* (and usually a י between the second and third root letters), it indicates the Causative Active – מַפְעִיל הִפְעִיל, while the Causative Passive Present has a *kubutz* or *kametz* under the מ prefix – מֻפְעַל הֻפְעַל.

- ❖ The הִתְ of the Reflexive in the past, becomes מִתְ in the present.

- ❖ To form the future tense of the five *binyanim* that have a מ prefix in the present tense, drop the מ prefix and replace it with the appropriate future tense letter א, ת, י or נ and keep the vowels as they were in the present tense.

- ❖ The sign of the present tense in the פָּעַל *binyan* is a *cholom* (ו) between the first and second root letters.

- ❖ The sign of the future tense of the פָּעַל *binyan,* is the prefix א, ת, י or נ with a *chirik,* and a *sheva nach* under the first root letter.

- ❖ The sign of the present tense of the נִפְעַל *binyan* is a נ prefix with a *chirik,* a *sheva nach* under the first root letter, and a *kametz* under the second root letter. The future tense of the נפעל *binyan* is unique as the prefix letter א, ת, י or נ must have a full vowel (long or short) and the first and second root letters must also have full vowels (long or short), with no *sheva* under the prefix letter or first two root letters.

- ❖ Only א,ת,י,נ,מ,ה may be prefix letters for verb roots.

Vocabulary for Dik Duk CD's

A

Ari-Arizal famous Rabbi
Aliya- going up- coming to Israel
Avodas "ה"- serving G-d
<u>Ashkanaz</u>- European

B

Baba myseh- white lie
Bircas cohanim- priestly blessings
Ba'al koreh- reader of sacred texts
B'reishis- Genesis
Ba'midbar- Numbers
Benching- prayer after eating bread
Ba'al Tschuva- religious returnee

C

Chiddish- unique understanding
Chumash-bible
Chutz La'aretz- out of Israel
Cantor- prayer leader
Chilazon- snail, source of blue thread
Chavar- associate- friend

D

Davakus le'Hashem- clinging to G-d
Daven- pray
Dafka- this and only this
Devorim- Deuteronomy

E

Eretz Yisroel- land of Israel

G

Gemorrah / Talmud- commentaries on written & oral law
Gerund- noun form of verb root
Ge'niza- burial place for documents with G-d's name

H

Ha'kaddosh baruch hu- G-d

I

Infix- letter between root letters

K

Kotel- western wall
Kabbalah- mystical teaching
Kosher- fitting (usually eat), can also be to do or say.

L

Loshon ha'kodesh- holy language Hebrew
LCD- Lowest Common Denominator

M

Machpala- Chevron burial tomb
Mishna- oral law

Midos- personality traits, behavioral characteristics
Mesorah- handed down tradition
Mishna brueur- legal codes
Mitzrayim- Egypt
Makor- base word form

N

Nikud- vowel

P

Pratim- details
Parchment- kosher animal skins to write on
Pesach- holiday of Exodus

R

Rashi- famous rabbinic commentator
Ramban- famous rabbinic authority
Rambam- famous rabbinic authority
Rebbi- rabbinic leader & author of Mishnayot

S

Schul- prayer house
Sefer Torah- bible scroll
Seforim- books
Sfard/sfardi- North Africa/Middle East
Shabbos- day of strict rest
Shalliach- messenger
Shema- Torah declaration of unity
Shemos- Exodus
Shiur- lesson/ class
Shmonei esrei- 19 blessings
Shoresh- root letter
Sofet letter- final letter
Shteig- learn strong, review

T

Tachlis- purpose
Tikun- fixing
Tatee- father
Tehilim- poems of King David
T'cheiles- blue color thread

V

Vayikra- Leviticus

Y

Yeshiva- Jewish house of study
Yom tov- holiday of rest

Z

Zohar- mystical text

9 781949 126075